JEFF DWYER

PELICAN PUBLISHING
NEW ORLEANS

ISBN 9781455628728

All images courtesy of the author unless otherwise noted.

Printed in the United States of America
Published by Pelican Publishing
New Orleans, LA
www.pelicanpub.com

To my mother, who always believed in ghosts…and in me.

CONTENTS

INTRODUCTION

Throughout history, islands have been viewed as intriguing and mysterious places. Their insular nature, surrounded by waters that may be calm and clear or impenetrable and threatening, sets them apart from the more familiar and comforting great land masses. The expanse of the intervening waters often does not affect our fascination with the island, nor does its size dispel the notion that the landmass is different, arousing our curiosity and triggering a desire to explore the place.

The effect of an island's isolation is sometimes minimal, but most often it is profound and may invoke notions of unseen barriers, shipwrecks, armed conflicts, and catastrophic events that killed many people. Suspicions run high of unmarked graveyards filled with bodies that emit paranormal energy surrounded by derelict structures that appear dangerous and foreboding. The impression of isolation creates a mystique that fills us with a sense of vulnerability to the unseen and leads naturally to the inescapable conclusion that something supernatural resides on the island. Rumors, legends, folklore of fatal disasters and horrendous deeds attract our attention, while the energy of the dead becomes a magnet that we cannot resist. The power of the attraction is always stronger when there is a widely accepted belief that the island is haunted.

Some haunted islands are popular destinations, attracting a vast array of visitors ranging from thrill-seekers and serious explorers to tourists who are non-believers of the paranormal or oblivious to the island's supernatural history. Alcatraz Island, in San Francisco Bay, and Corregidor, at the entrance to Manila Bay, are visited by more than 1 million people each year. Others, such as Poveglia, in the Venetian Lagoon of northern Italy, and Daksa, in the Croatian part of the Adriatic Sea, have a history so horrendous that local governments deny access.

Haunted islands tend to have many common characteristics, including treacherous currents or strong winds that make approaches by water dangerous. Steep beaches, rocky headlands, or unsafe piers may add to the challenges of getting safely on shore. Because of age and exposure to environmental stresses, haunted structures on the island may be unsafe or conceal hazards such as broken glass, protruding nails, weak floorboards, and even unexploded ordnance. Neglected graveyards and sites of tragic events, such as executions or massacres, may also contain these hazards. Added to all of that, spirits may reside in these places that may be angry and belligerent toward unwanted visitors. Some haunted islands may be quite the opposite. Locations in Hawaii, the San Francisco Bay, Puget Sound, the Great Lakes, Southern California, and New England are easily accessed, safe for tourists and paranormal explorers alike, and offer amenities that make the visit quite comfortable.

Whatever the objective of an island ghost hunt, the allure of an offshore location and a tantalizing history can lead to an exciting adventure and productive investigation. Haunted islands often present a vibrant amalgam of a fascinating history, folklore, and superstition that may be irresistible, especially to those who seek paranormal experiences.

The islands in San Francisco Bay comprise a collection of locations intensely haunted by the spirits of deceased people who lived dramatic and sometimes dangerous lives as heroes, criminals, victims, or innocent participants in the history of the region that sometimes took dark turns or placed them in unanticipated disasters. The islands presented in this book—Alcatraz, Alameda, Mare Island, Angel Island, Yerba Buena Island, and Treasure Island—are haunted by the spirits of people who faced criminal violence, environmental disasters, fatal illness from epidemics, and massive explosions triggered by sabotage and negligence, as well as many others who died while devoted to duty, family, or the welfare of others. To understand their history, we must understand the haunted history of the San Francisco Bay Area.

HAUNTED SAN FRANCISCO BAY AREA

Native Americans who inhabited the Bay Area region for thousands of years or more have left remnants of their existence in hundreds of locations surrounding the bay. Shell mounds containing tools, jewelry, and remains of the deceased have been preserved as monuments, while many others rest under city streets and modern buildings. Discovery and desecration of their graves during construction projects have led to reports of spirit activity and disturbing paranormal events.

Since the 1770s, the region has been populated with people from a variety of cultures who experienced tremendous changes in their lives. Changes and challenges that were, at times, overwhelming were created by transition of the region in 1820 from a Spanish colony to a province under the tenuous control of Mexico and then, in 1846, to a nearly lawless American territory. The calamity of the Gold Rush from 1849 to 1858 brought thousands of people to the San Francisco Bay Area before they embarked for the gold fields and diggings of the Sierra Nevada, creating even more turmoil in the region. The growing wealth of the region's cities and towns, and admission of California to the Union in 1850 as the thirty-first state, did little to dampen criminal activity, reduce civil disobedience, dispel racism, or civilize those who had abandoned the best qualities of their character to seek quick riches. Other cataclysmic changes were brought about by armed conflicts, including skirmishes between Indians and white settlers, Yankees who confronted Mexican soldiers in the 1846 Bear Flag Revolt, and San Francisco's vigilante mobs and criminals.

Epidemics that swept through the Bay Area brought tragedy to many families, ending lives at a young age and filling many pioneer cemeteries. In 1855, the SS *Sam* arrived in San Francisco Bay carrying immigrants from the Far East. Within a few days, a cholera epidemic broke out, eventually filling several makeshift cemeteries. In 1900, ships that moored at San Francisco's piers discharged rats infected with bubonic plague. The epidemic that followed was not eradicated until 1905. Fear that the accumulation of many unburied corpses would prolong the epidemic prompted city leaders to establish new cemeteries far beyond city limits. Graves of plague victims were exhumed from city cemeteries and the bodies transported to Colma and other locations on the San Francisco peninsula. The Spanish flu epidemic of 1918 that killed 100 million people worldwide left 2,220 dead in San Francisco. In fascinating cemeteries, such as the Mission Dolores graveyard in San Francisco, the National Cemetery of the Presidio of San Francisco, and the Columbarium of San Francisco, some grave markers list specific epidemics as cause of death. Many also reveal that death came at a young age, creating spirits that have yet to let go and move on.

In the 1880s, San Jose and Fremont suffered devastating fires, but they were minor compared to more contemporary disasters. Following the San Francisco Earthquake of 1906, ruptured gas mains created thirty fires that swept through the city accounting for 90 percent of the destruction and causing more than three thousand deaths; 490 city blocks were affected, culminating in the destruction of twenty-five thousand buildings including a San Francisco landmark, the Palace Hotel.

On October 17, 1989, the Loma Prieta earthquake killed sixty-three people while leaving as many as twelve thousand people homeless after fires swept through San Francisco's Marina District. Much of the destruction in the neighborhood was attributed to the construction of houses on rubble from the 1906 earthquake.

The Oakland Hills Firestorm of 1991 served as a gruesome reminder that even modern construction is not immune to the kinds of fires that destroyed many gold rush–era towns in regions surrounding the Bay Area. The Oakland Hills Fire killed 25 people and consumed 3,354 single-family homes and 437 apartments. Many who died in the firestorm were overcome by heat and smoke as they fought flames with garden hoses and other means. Others were caught by the fiery blast as they attempted to navigate roads obscured by smoke and burning debris.

Fires that swept through rural and suburban areas of the late nineteenth century also destroyed thousands of wooden grave markers in town cemeteries. During ensuing periods of rapid rebuilding and expansion in Oakland, San Francisco, San Jose, and Palo Alto, spirits became restless when buildings were constructed over their unmarked graves. In the 1990s, during construction of parks, homes, businesses, and streets, several graves were discovered and inadvertently desecrated, leading to reports of ghostly activity in modern structures. Most recently, graves have been discovered during sewer reconstruction under the streets of Los Gatos, in Fairfield, and in the Presidio of San Francisco.

With three major airports and numerous military facilities in the Bay Area, aviation and naval disasters have become a prominent part of local history. On July 17, 1944, the Port Chicago Naval Magazine was nearly wiped from the face of the earth by a massive explosion that sank two cargo ships laden with munitions and several smaller vessels and killed more than three hundred dock workers. It has been estimated that ten thousand tons of explosives were ignited by a heavy shell or bomb that had been dropped on a steel deck. The force of the 10:19 p.m. explosion awoke people in Oakland, more than twenty miles away. Debris weighing as much as two hundred pounds was blasted as far as five miles from the site of the disaster.

On February 11, 1968, two U.S. Navy aviators died when their T-33b jet departed from the Alameda Naval Air Station and hit the Bay Bridge. Tragedy struck the bridge again in 1989 when the Loma Prieta earthquake caused part of the roadbed to collapse, killing two people. The nearby Cypress Freeway collapsed, adding forty-two to the death toll.

On February 7, 1973, a Navy Corsair jet fighter crashed into an apartment building a few blocks from my home in Alameda. The 8:13 p.m. crash was heard all over the island city. Aside from the pilot, ten people were killed, while twenty-six were injured. The crash site, at 1814 Central Avenue, has been rebuilt, and nothing remains to mark the disaster except the spirits that walk through the new building. Another airplane crash, at Sun Valley Mall in Concord on December 23, 1985, left seven dead. Environmental remnants of this disaster have been detected by psychics on the third floor of the mall.

Several disasters dating before 1920 have contributed to the restless spirits of the Bay Area. These include the San Francisco cable car explosion of February 1887, Alameda Masonic temple gas explosion of 1904, the sinking of the ferryboat *Contra Costa* in 1859, the fire aboard the steamship *Columbia* in 1907, and the Mare Island (Vallejo) Navy Yard explosion in 1892.

All of these tragic events add to the region's paranormal legacy and have left powerful emotional imprints created by spirits of the dearly departed that felt a need to stay on. A common factor in the creation of a ghost is the loss of life by a sudden, violent event, often at a young age, leaving the spirit with an inextinguishable desire to achieve their life's objectives or with a sense of obligation to offer protection to a particular place or person.

Some ghosts remain on the earthly plane for revenge or to provide guidance for someone still alive. Many of those who came to California for gold were caught up in their dreams of great wealth but met with only frustration and failure before dying alone and in poverty. Their restless spirits still roam the streets of Gold Rush–era towns such as Benicia and Clayton and the back roads of rural areas searching for the elusive yellow metal.

Communities of the San Francisco Bay Area have had their share of criminal activities and social injustice. From October 1966 to May 1981, Bay Area communities lived in the fear of the Zodiac Killer. Credited with forty-nine possible victims, this mass murderer has yet to be caught. The Zodiac left victims in Vallejo, Lake Berryessa, Presidio Heights in San Francisco, Benicia, Richmond, and other areas that may include four western states.

On July 1, 1993, Gian Luigi Ferri entered the law offices of Pettit and Martin at 101 California Street in San Francisco and opened fire with two pistols. After the smoke cleared, six lay injured among eight who were killed. Ferri shot himself as police arrived at the scene.

Ghost hunters who are fascinated by criminals will want to visit Alcatraz Island. Before the tiny island in San Francisco Bay was transformed into a prison, "the Rock" was known by Native Americans as a place occupied by evil spirits. In spite of Indian legends, the U.S. Army established a fort on the island in1850. During construction between the wharf and guardhouse, a landslide buried two men and led to renewed warnings that the place was haunted by evil spirits. During the next fifty years, an untold number of prisoners—deserters, Southern sympathizers of the Civil War era, criminals, and escapees from other prisons—died in their cells. In 1907, the Army vacated the island as a Bay Area defense installation, making way for its transformation to the Western U.S. Military Prison. Ultimately, the place became a federal prison for some of America's most famous criminals, including Al Capone, Public Enemy No. 1 Alvin Karpis, George "Machine Gun" Kelly, and the Birdman of Alcatraz, Robert Stroud. It is believed that during its twenty-nine years of operation, no prisoners escaped from the Rock. Official records reveal that thirty-six men were involved in fourteen attempts. Six escapees were shot and killed on the rocks at water's edge, while two were unaccounted for and believed drowned in the bay.

From one of the most horrendous cult-related crimes in American history, 412 victims are interred at Oakland's Evergreen Cemetery. On November 18, 1978, at urging of cult leader Jim Jones, 918 people died by mass suicide in a Guyana village. Since many of the victims were once residents of the Bay Area, a large plot was made available for burial in the East Bay. Electronic voice phenomena (EVP) and other paranormal experiences have been reported at this location.

The activities of criminals have produced many used, abused, confused, and forlorn spirits that may remain with us after their death. The spirits of these victims may still seek lost dreams while they remain attached to what little they gained during their difficult lives. Many ghosts harbor deep resentment, pain, or a desire to complete their unfinished business, and they still roam the darkened halls of courthouses, jails, prisons, hotels, theater, cemeteries, modern buildings, and many other places throughout the region that are accessible to the public.

WHAT IS A GHOST?

A ghost is some aspect of the personality, spirit, consciousness, energy, mind, intelligence, or soul that remains after the body dies. When any these are detected by the living—through sight, sound, odor, tactile sensations, or movement of objects—parapsychologists consider the experience to be a paranormal encounter. How the ghost manifests is not completely understood, but there are many useful theories that help us understand ghostly behavior. There seems to be a close association between aspects of the entity's life and the modalities it uses to manifest on our plane of existence. These include a sudden, traumatic death; strong ties to loved ones who survived the entity or to a particular place; unfinished business; strong emotions such as hatred and anger; or a desire for revenge.

Ghosts differ from other paranormal phenomena by their display of intelligent interaction with a witness or the environment. This includes interaction with the living by touching, speaking, gestures, or facial expressions; movement of objects; sounds such as tapping in response to questions; or creation of sounds or electronic analogs on audio recorders and light anomalies on image media.

Ghosts manifest on our plane of existence for many reasons. They may want to:

- protect a cherished possession such as a book collection, art, weapons, jewelry, money, and so on
- protect a cherish place such as a house, office, lab, workshop, and more
- watch over loved ones
- enlist the help of a living person to discover something hidden
- explore their curiosity about the fate of people or a particular place or object
- offer guidance to family, friends, or business partners
- seek revenge

There may be other reasons, but these motivations explain most spirit activity. Most spirits are place-bound rather than people-bound. That is, most are attached to, or drawn to a particular place such as a house, office, airplane, boat, movie theater, and so on.

In terms of manifestation, ghosts interact with our environment in a variety of ways that may have something to do with the strength of their personality, desire to communicate, or level of confusion concerning their transformation by death. The talents or skills they possessed in life, their personal objectives, or frustrations arising from the end of life may underlie their efforts in getting our attention. Some ghosts create odors, particularly those associated with their habits, such as cigar smoke or signature perfumes. Many reports from credible witnesses mention the odors of tobacco, oranges, and hemp as most common.

A ghost may be present if an unseen entity interacts with the environment by performing purposeful activity or responds to a change in the environment. Unexplained movement of objects such as books, a pipe, eyeglasses, tools, weapons, doorknobs, bedding, and more that cannot be attributed to normal or natural processes often indicates the presence of a ghost.

Some ghosts have been known to rearrange furniture, room decorations, or the like to suit their preferences. If new objects are placed in a ghost's favorite room, they may be found moved outside the room, broken, or hidden in another location. Common ghostly activities are movement of a rocking chair, turning of doorknobs, activation of light switches and electronic equipment such as TVs, and disheveling bedding.

Ghosts like to knock over stacks of cards or coins, turn doorknobs, scatter matchsticks, and move your keys. For many, it appears easy to manipulate light switches and TV remotes, open and close windows and doors, or push chairs around. Some ghosts have the power to throw objects, pull pictures from walls, or move heavy items. As a rule, ghosts cannot tolerate disturbances within the place they haunt. If you tilt a wall-mounted picture, the ghost will set it straight. Obstacles placed in the ghost's path may be pushed aside.

Ghosts can also create changes in the physical qualities of an environment. Ice-cold breezes and unexplained gusts of wind are often the first signs that a ghost is present. Moving or stationary cold spots, with temperatures several degrees below surrounding areas, have been detected with reliable instruments. Temperature changes sometimes occur with a feeling that the atmosphere has thickened as if the room was suddenly filled with unseen people.

Ghosts may create images on still cameras and video recorders such as luminous fogs, balls of light called orbs, streaks of light, or the partial outline of body parts. Thousands of images reputed to be paranormal may be viewed on the Internet, but modern digital images are easily edited and make it difficult to find convincing proof of ghostly activity.

In many cases, the ghost's primary desire is to communicate. Sounds, including voice messages, may be detected with an audio recorder. Ghosts may speak to the living to warn of an unforeseen accident or disaster, protect a cherished place or object, give advice, or express their love, anger, remorse, or disappointment. Ghost hunters have recorded greetings, warnings, screams, sobbing, and expressions of love.

Humanoid images of ghosts are the prized objective of most ghost hunters, but they are seldom observed. When such images occur, they are often partial, revealing only a head and torso with an arm or two. Feet are seldom seen. Full-body apparitions are extremely rare. Some ghost hunters have seen ethereal, fully transparent forms that are barely discernible. Others report seeing ghosts that appear as solid as a living being.

The foremost objective of most paranormal investigators is to observe an apparition. Unfortunately, the sighting of an apparition is rare. There have been many instances when ghosts appear completely lifelike, however. More commonly, spirits appear as partial apparitions—a hand, a foot, or head—possibly because they are confused about their transition from life to death or they lack the energy to create an image of their entire body. Ghosts that possess little energy may manifest as an amorphous cloud, a shadow that barely resembles the human form, or streaks of light. Round disks of light captured on photographic media called "orbs" have been accepted as evidence of spirit presence. Experts agree, however, that the vast majority of orb photographs are the result of operating characteristics of the camera, not ghostly activity.

The best theory to explain the apparent ability of ghosts to communicate with the living is through telepathy, a process that not only enables the perception of spoken words but also creates images of apparitions, tactile sensations such as touching and cool breezes, and nonvocal sounds such as footsteps. It can also generate perceptions of fear, anxiety, depression, pain, presence of an unseen being, and an awareness of being watched.

It is challenging to understand the underlying physical or psychic process that enables telepathic communication, projected from the consciousness of a dead person to a living being, because there is very little scientific fact to confirm any one of several compelling theories. It likely involves some kind of psychic energy release or flux, or manipulation of existing electromagnetic fields by the spirit. Some parapsychologists call this psychic phenomenon "psi energy." Psi energy may alter electromagnetic fields, enabling transfer of information from a spirit entity to the living brain.

WHY DO GHOSTS REMAIN AT A PARTICULAR PLACE?

Ghosts remain in a particular place because they are emotionally attached to a room, a building, or special surroundings that profoundly affected them during their lives, or to activities or events that played a role in their death. Upon transitioning to death, the ghost may remain in a place that it knew, while alive, as safe and comfortable.

It is widely believed that death and sudden transition from the physical world confuses a ghost. He or she remains in familiar or emotionally stabilizing surroundings to ease the strain. A place-bound ghost is most likely to occur when a violent death occurred with great emotional anguish. Ghosts may linger in a house, barn, cemetery, factory, or store waiting for a loved one or anyone familiar who might help them deal with their new level of existence. Some ghosts wander through buildings or a confined area within a forest, on bridges, or alongside particular sections of a road, but they rarely travel far.

Fear of the unknown path ahead motivates some ghosts to stay as close to familiar surroundings or people as possible. The possibility of judgment by higher beings, facing other spirits that they hurt or mistreated during life, or having to recognize the errors of one's life may be too much for some spirits. Earth-bound spirits motivated by fear can be difficult to banish, but background research may provide paranormal investigators with information about crimes, wrong-doing or reprehensible personality flaws that may enhance the effectiveness of banishing rituals.

IMPRINTS AND RESIDUALS

Imprints and *residuals* are terms that refer to the same type of paranormal phenomenon, one that has nothing to do with a ghost. Noted author and respected researcher Loyd Auerbach explains that the lack of intelligent interaction with a witness or the environment requires us to forego a claim that we've had an encounter with a ghost and consider the experience a perception of imprint or residual phenomena. An imprint is the result of intense, repetitive emotions experienced by a living person during an event or activity at a specific location. It may be created by a single event or the same event performed repetitively. The energy of the experience is embedded in the local environment much like the electronic audio signals are embedded on a recording media. I have estimated that 80 percent to 90 percent of paranormal experiences are perception of imprints, not ghostly encounters.

Typically, the imprint contain the energy of human experience such as fear, joy, grief, or anger. If the principal feature of this phenomenon is an inanimate object, it is called a phantom. Imprints may create a variety of experiences in five primary categories:

1. OLFACTORY: the perception of odors or fragrances that may include perfume, flowers, animals, fruit such as oranges, hemp tobacco, rotting meat, sour milk, horses, or smoke.
2. AUDITORY: sounds such as vocalizations, including spoken words, humming, whistling, yawning, or sobbing, as well as nonvocal sounds such as musical instruments, footsteps, gunshots, horse's hooves, slamming doors, or breaking glass. These sounds may be detectable only through recording equipment, or they may be heard through the normal hearing mechanisms of the human ear.
3. VISUAL: amorphous shapes, humanoid shadows, partial apparitions, or full-bodied apparitions. These may be seen by one witness but not seen by another, suggesting a psychic process or individual differences in sensitivity.
4. PHOTOGRAPHIC: paranormal images (those lacking a "normal" explanation) not seen with the eyes when imaging equipment was used but found in still pictures or video, film or digital—including orbs, streaks of light, unexplained shadows, or humanoid shapes.
5. TACTILE: in some instances, energy emanates from imprints that creates bizarre impressions of being touched or crowded by the close presence of an unseen being or other perceptions including thickened air or even cold spots.
6. CHARACTERISTICS: imprints and residuals may appear similar or even identical to ghostly activity. Imprint phenomena implies that there is no consciousness present that is responsible for the paranormal activity. Imprints may be sufficiently unsettling, however, that some witnesses will suffer from anxiety or sleep disturbances or become fearful.

Witnesses of imprint phenomena have reported seeing pale, transparent images of a deceased person walking in hallways, climbing stairs, sitting in rocking chairs, or sitting on airplanes, trains, buses, and even in restaurants. Some humanoid images have been seen sleeping in beds, hanging by a rope from a tree, or walking through walls. Some humanoid images appear completely lifelike, while other are barely discernible, fully transparent, and limited to a hand, a pair of boot-clad legs, or a head.

Imprints tend to be associated with a specific place or object, not a particular person. Humanoid figures tend to perform a repetitive task or activity. Sometimes the imprint is so repetitive that witnesses feel as though they are watching a video loop that plays the same brief scene over and over. A good example is that of a deceased grandmother that makes appearances seated in her favorite rocking chair. If the chair does not move and the ghostly image appears not to notice witnesses or changes in the local environment, this is an imprint, not a ghost. Typically, a figure will perform the same repetitive task or activity without variation for a few seconds, rarely more than a minute.

Olfactory perceptions may range from the engaging fragrance of expensive perfume to the horrible stench of rotted meat. It is often useful to identify the fragrance, such as magnolia or Chanel No 5 perfume. The identity of a fragrance might, for example, be linked with background research that indicates a former female occupant of a house loved magnolias or used Chanel perfume. This link can lead to identification of the person whose emotional experience created the imprint. Offensive odors could be the result of illness that preceded death or the process of decomposition that occurred when a dead body was left undiscovered for a long time.

Auditory imprints form the majority of non-ghostly paranormal experiences. Sensitives may hear psychically, or with normal hearing processes, human vocalizations, musical instruments, gunshots, footsteps, the movement of horse-drawn carriages, slamming doors, and more. Auditory imprints are often readily captured on recording devices. Thousands of high-quality recordings known as electronic voice phenomena (EVP) and electronic audio phenomena (EAP) may be found on the internet.

The most compelling imprint phenomenon is the sighting of a humanoid apparition. These may appear as dark shadows, figures composed of white smoke or fog, transparent partial body parts, transparent whole-body figures, and lifelike bodies.

Images generated by imprint phenomena and captured on still or video image media may range from clearly humanoid to amorphous light anomalies. The latter have been described as streaks, fogs, haze, or a disk of light dubbed an "orb." Light anomalies are most often generated by operating deficiencies of the photographic device, but they may be paranormal if corroborating evidence is obtained such as an audio recording.

Like a file recorded on a computer disk, the recording may be quite durable, lasting decades or even centuries. Visitors to European battlefields have experienced the sounds and sights of military conflicts that occurred more than one thousand years earlier. Standing amid warring knights and charging Roman legions, astonished witnesses remained untouched and apparently unnoticed, ruling out the possibility that the encounter was ghostly.

There is a lot of evidence that living people can "trigger" an environmental imprints to "play" by visiting the particular site, touching an object that was a key element of the event, or psychically connecting with the event. The location of strong environmental imprints can also be discovered through devices such as dowsing roads, crystal pendulums, and electromagnetic field detectors. Higher magnetic field readings have been found at locations where psychics frequently experience imprints.

CHAPTER 1
ALAMEDA

For nearly 3,500 years, the low peninsula along the eastern shore of San Francisco Bay was home to the Ohlone Indians. During this long occupation of mudflats and land that came to be known as the city of Alameda, mounds of discarded shells, tools, and even bodies of the deceased were deposited and eventually covered by storms and floods, as well as the growth of large groves of poplar trees. When the Spanish arrived in 1776, the land was unoccupied, but they noticed the groves of poplar trees and so named the place Alameda. Soon after Spain relinquished northern California to the Mexican government in 1820, Luis Peralta was awarded a land grant of thirty-five square miles that included Alameda. By 1851, the Peralta family had sold several parcels of the vast land grant. One of them encompassed the low peninsula on which the city of Alameda was founded. The gold rush that extended into the 1850s and rapid development of San Francisco in the 1860s brought wealth to the city's early residents, who established farms and docks that serviced the Alaska packers fishing fleets.

Incorporated as a city in 1872, the town became a charming enclave of Victorian-style mansions and broad streets. From 1874 to 1902, the broad creek separating the town from Oakland was widened and deepened to accommodate hundreds of three-masted sailing ships, further enhancing the character of the town as a major shipping center and wealthy bedroom community.

The first bridge spanning the creek between Alameda and Oakland was built in 1871. Additional connections were established in 1900, and in 1926, a "tube" was built conveying cars and trucks under the estuary between Oakland and Alameda.

World War I brought industrial development that included steel mills and shipbuilding facilities. An airport opened at the west end of the town in 1928 that provided China clipper service by Pan American seaplanes. In 1935, development of the Naval Air Station started by filling tidal mud flats with dredged sand, creating nearly one thousand acres of usable land. Development of the base proceeded rapidly as World War II started, and the town's population doubled as its character changed to that of a major Navy community.

Early in the twentieth century, several impressive civic buildings were constructed, including the city hall (1895–1901), library (1903), veterans' memorial building (1928), theater (1932), U.S. post office (1912), and high school (1926).

With the closure of the naval air station in 1997 and relocation of many heavy industries, Alameda's renown as a bedroom community for the Bay Area's major cities was restored and greatly enhanced. Many of the old Victorian mansions and modest houses have been restored and rarely sell for less than $1 million.

GHOST OF THE BALLET DANCER

Alameda High School
2200 Central Avenue
510-337-7022

Old theaters and performance venues tend to be haunted, and the huge auditorium of Alameda High School is no exception. Considered one of the most beautiful high schools in California, the cornerstone of the Neoclassical Revival structure was laid in 1902; years later the school received city, state, and national landmark status.

Construction of the school's three large buildings, encompassing 100,000 square feet, was not completed until 1926. An impressive collection of ten Ionic columns stand at the main entrance, which leads directly into the foyer and grand auditorium. Known as the Kofman Auditorium, it seats 2,300 with a stage sixty feet wide. The backstage spans forty feet and may

Ghost of the ballet dancer, captured on the stage at Alameda High School.

extend into the gymnasium when sets and casts require extra space. Over the backstage, a huge collection of backdrops and lighting gear are stored overhead by a pulley system. This array of ropes and spars once offered a young woman the equipment she needed to commit suicide on stage.

Many students and faculty at AHS know the story of the stage ghost, but no one can specify the date of the tragic event or reveal the name of the deceased. Apparently, the girl was a ballet dancer who frequently performed and practiced on the stage. Some reports suggest that she fell and accidentally hanged herself by becoming entangled in stage ropes of lifting gear for light fixtures. Having been a performer on the stage many times, I can affirm that this is not likely. The lifting gear that hangs over the stage is at least thirty feet above the stage surface. The more widely circulated story is that, having learned she was pregnant, she decided to end her life in a place where she had experienced the greatest joy. Reports state that she was found with laces from her ballet shoes tied around her neck. The possibility that she was murdered is not mentioned in online reports of this tragic event.

People who have seen the ghost of the ballet dancer have nicknamed her "Bubbles" because she appear surrounded by orbs that emit scintillating light. She has been spotted center stage, backstage, and in some of the dressing rooms. Aside from her apparition, people report hearing unexplained sounds such as the soft patter of ballet shoes on the stage's surface, humming melodies that accompany ballet, and heavy breathing.

The date of this tragic event is uncertain, but it likely took place before 1960. I interviewed people who attended AHS between 1960 and 1986, and none recalled a suicide in Kofman Auditorium. A search of the archives of the local newspaper, the *Alameda Times Star* (1877–2011), failed to yield any corroborating documentation of this ghost story. People who have seen the ghostly ballet dancer, however, are adamant that they have witnessed a ghost.

Aside from a ghost, there are hundreds of paranormal imprints on the campus of the old high school. While standing at the huge metal doors at the main entrance, bursts of unexplained sounds are often heard that include band music and cheering students (for decades, pregame rallies were staged on the steps of the main entrance).

Some famous people attended Alameda High School, including Jim Morrison of the Doors, cookie empire creator Debbie Fields, Manson family murder victim Sharon Tate, Oakland Raiders tackle Rich Zecker, two-time World Series champion Andy Carey, San Francisco Giants shortstop Chris Speier, and Emmy-winning producer Hank Saroyan.

A GATHERING OF EAGLES

Eagles Hall
2305 Alameda Avenue

Serving as a most favored gathering spot for member of the Fraternal Order of Eagles for more than a century, this venerable old building is a hot spot of paranormal activity. Well documented by an exceptional team of investigators, the Alameda Paranormal Researchers, the place seems to be a magnet for members who died elsewhere but preferred to socialize with deceased friends rather than move onward to the great unknown.

Staff of the Eagles Hall have learned to live with the strange things that happen in virtually every room. Bartender Ernie Estoy has reported his kitchen radio turns on and off when the lights are turned on in morning. He has also heard the rocking, shuffling sound of tables and stomping feet on the floor above the kitchen when he is certain that there is no one else in the building.

Eagles trustee Bryan Ashton has seen a full-bodied apparition. While looking up the stairs past the locked accordion gate, Bryan observed a tall, dark figure standing on the mid-floor landing. Upon making eye contact, the ghostly figure dashed up the stairs and disappeared behind a wall.

The Eagles Hall in Alameda may be haunted by former members.

APR team member Ying Liu entered the foyer one afternoon and spotted a colleague, cameraman Cody, kneeling on the stairs. His upper body was concealed by a wall, but his body, from hips to toes, appeared completely lifelike. She greeted her colleague only to watch the image fade as the real Cody entered the foyer through a doorway.

In many areas of the hall, the fragrance of roses and stale food is perceived by many staff and visitors. The odor is especially strong in the hallway that serves as a coat room. Some have described the odor as "old lady perform," while others find it pleasant. Typically, the fragrance appears in a narrow "cell," manifesting and dissipating suddenly. An odor described as that of a foul body also occurs in several locations, perhaps an imprint from the days when bathing was a once-per-week habit.

EVP captured in the main hall include, "This house is haunted" and "I live here." In the attic, while trustee Bryan Ashton leafed through century-old ledgers, the APR team recorded, "I'm the worst."

In 2019, exceptional psychic June Ahern visited the Eagles Hall and perceived the presence of some fascinating ghosts. June made contact with a young girl, about seventeen to nineteen years old, who died more than a century earlier while residing at a farm or ranch on land now occupied by the building. Dressed in a long white dress, June learned that the girl is confused and does not know where she should go. As the psychic investigation continued, June perceived the name Silva or Silvius. Historical research by APR revealed that the Silva ranch was located in this general vicinity and that two young girls died there. Emma, age seventeen, died on September 13, 1895, while Emily, aged nineteen, died on August 1, 1905. June felt that the presence of one of the girls in the hall was tied to a cemetery or mortuary that may have been located on Alameda Avenue.

There is considerable doubt that the psychic impression of a cemetery is accurate. It is highly unlikely that conventional cemeteries would be created in Alameda because the water table is only six feet below ground surface. However, there may have been some graves established on nineteenth-century family farms that became neglected and covered by construction of streets and buildings. Maps of Alameda in 1878 and 1908 show no cemeteries. There is a mortuary a few blocks from the hall, at 1415 Oak Street, next to a church built in 1908.

June's psychic investigation turned darker as she perceived the presence of a spirit described as "gloomy" with a criminal history. A group picture of Eagles members taken prior to 1920, hanging in the social room, includes the image of a man in top hat and tuxedo named George Costello. Bryan believes that this is the man he saw on the stairs. Nicknamed "Top Hat," this spirit was perceived as a bad man. Research revealed that George Costello was a bank robber who was hanged at San Quentin on December 13, 1929. Clearly, George has returned to the Eagles Hall seeking the companionship of his friends.

June Ahern has also perceived several spirits in the bar, chatting incessantly. One of these spirits is named Albert, but the roster of member lists many with that given name, precluding any specific identification. In the great hall, a male spirit that died of a heart attack resides there.

When I was I high school, I walked by the Eagles Hall twice each day. The place always looked mysterious to me because of the dark windows and lack of any kind of activity at the place. The building also had a cold presence, quite different from many of the old buildings on the block. Added to that, if I happened to pass close to the front stairs, I often felt a strange vibe that left me feeling that I should not get to close to the door. Friends told me that the place was haunted by a mean ghost. Thanks to June Ahern and APR, we now know that there was, indeed, a ghost there who was a criminal when alive.

View the Alameda Paranormal Researchers investigation, featuring psychic June Ahern and ghost hunter Sommer Jonez, on YouTube.

USS *HORNET*

Former Alameda Naval Air Station
Atlantic Avenue Entrance
707 West Hornet Avenue
510-521-8484
www.uss-hornet.org

It has been said that all ships are haunted, especially those that served in combat. Fear and anger experienced by dedicated crew members during battles would produce intense environmental imprints detectable as paranormal activity. Accidents in engine rooms; fires in fueling stations; explosions in ammunition holds and in gun turrets; bullets, shells, and torpedoes fired by the enemy; and aircraft crashes on a flight deck would naturally produce ghosts confused by the end of life while still feeling the need to remain on duty. Many of the dead would be young men, fiercely loyal to their ship and shipmates and so devoted to service to their country that they would not let death keep them from defending their homeland and defeating an enemy. The World War II aircraft carrier USS *Hornet* has a history that includes the horror of battle, tragedy of countless accidents,

The USS *Hornet* is one of the most haunted warships in America.

misfortune of numerous fatal illnesses, and overwhelming personal stress and mental anguish for many crew members. It isn't any wonder that the USS *Hornet* is one of the most haunted ships in America.

It was commissioned on November 29, 1943, and sent to the South Pacific to avenge its lost namesake, the aircraft carrier *Hornet* that was sunk by the Japanese in 1942 at Guadalcanal. Pilots flying from its deck sank 73 Japanese ships totaling 1,269,710 tons and destroyed 1,410 enemy aircraft. It was a key element in every amphibious landing after March 1944 and is credited with initiating the attack on the Japanese battleship *Yamato*, flagship of the fleet that attacked Pearl Harbor. During the bloody battles of Okinawa and Iwo Jima, the *Hornet* came under heavy attack fifty-nine times, sustaining severe battle damage but always remaining seaworthy and capable of aircraft operations. This combat record was not accomplished without considerable loss of crew. During twenty-seven years of service, more than 300 crew members died aboard this ship. Flight deck operations resulted in the decapitation of at least 3 crewmen by aircraft arresting cables. More than 30 sailors were killed by contact with aircraft propellers, while an unknown number were ingested by jet engine intake vents or burned by jet exhaust. More than 50 aircraft have crashed on the *Hornet*'s flight deck, killing air crew and flight deck workers. Aside from combat and accidents, long voyages severely stressed some crew members, leaving the *Hornet* with the dubious distinction of having the highest suicide rate of any ship in the U.S. Navy.

The last mission of this warship was a peaceful one, however. On July 24, 1969, it recovered the Apollo 11 astronauts upon their return from the moon. The nine-hundred-foot-long ship was decommissioned in 1979 and sat many years awaiting restoration. It was during this time that caretakers began noticing strange sounds and other odd events. At times, when no other living soul was aboard the old ship, watchmen heard loud tapping sounds reverberating through the steel hull. Heavy steel doors would slam shut or swing open. The possibility that these events could result from movement of the ship was dismissed, for the forty-two-thousand-ton vessel sat in placid, protected waters at Hunter's Point Naval Shipyard off San Francisco. Wind and tide could not cause rocking or other motions of the huge ship.

After the old *Hornet* opened as a museum in August 1998, staff members who continued the restoration and maintenance of the ship noticed the slamming doors, movement of objects, and the sounds of footsteps on the metal deck. Suspicions that the old ship was haunted spread quickly and

Infrared image of the ghost of a Navy firefighter in the *Hornet*'s engine room.

attracted the attention of paranormal investigators and TV producers. The *Hornet* has been featured in several movies, including *XXX: State of the Union*, and TV shows such as *JAG*. The *Hornet* has been featured in numerous paranormal shows, including *Sightings*, *Scariest Places on Earth*, and *Ghost Hunters*. Psychics such as Sylvia Brown have visited the ship and affirmed that the Gray Lady is indeed haunted. Some paranormal investigators believe that there may be as many as three hundred ghosts on this ship.

The USS *Hornet* has been investigated by several paranormal organizations, including Ghost Trackers, The Atlantic Paranormal Society (TAPS), Sonoma SPIRIT (headed by Jackie Ganiy), and the *Ghost Adventures* crew.

In 2010, the cast of the hit TV show *Ghost Adventures* investigated the *Hornet* with my colleague Nancy Bowman and discovered several hot spots of paranormal activity. In the ship's brig, or jail, Nancy and host Zak Bagans perceived an unseen entity pushing them close to the cell's bars. EVP recorded at this place captured a male voice saying, "Help me." Another recording including the command, "Get out!" and a male voice saying, "Bullnose."

In the ship's surgery center, Nancy perceived an operating table covered with blood. Audio recordings captured the sound of heavy footsteps leading from the operating room to the sick bay. In the sick bay, Nancy reported an earlier experience in which she saw the apparition of a burn victim while perceiving a foul odor from the wounds. EVP also included "Get up" and the statement "I was hurt." While lying in one of the beds, investigator Nick Groff felt his skin become hot, as though he suffered burns, and uncomfortable needle pricks in his arm.

At the head of the ship, an area known as the forecastle, the apparition of a sailor has been spotted hanging from a rope. The name of this unfortunate man has never been disclosed, but many staff of the ship have spotted the apparition, which is likely an imprint.

The most active haunted area of the *Hornet* is the gallery. Witnesses reported pots flying off the wall, trays pushed to the floor, and a bottle of soap thrown at a docent. EVP recorded in this area include "I'll get you" and Run." The disturbing activity in this spot has been attributed to an angry cook, who may have been abused by sailors who did not like the food.

Since the *Hornet* is berthed in my hometown, I've investigated ghostly activity on the ship many times. There are numerous dark passageways, dimly lit rooms, and dark spaces on a ship this size, but I've seen the most vivid apparitions in the well-lit sick bay. I've spotted the ghosts of sailors resting in the berths and lying unconscious on the operating table. I've also seen ghostly physicians and corpsmen moving around the sick bay. Other hot spots for ghostly activity are the pilots' ready room and the chapel.

During some of my visits to the old warship, I performed dowsing rod sessions to communicate with the souls on board. These sessions revealed that there are several ghosts on board that died elsewhere. I learned that sailors and aviators who served on other Navy ships and died after living a long life with a lengthy retirement found their way to the *Hornet* to spend years or decades in the company of other naval personnel. I also contacted a friend from my high school days who died in Vietnam while serving as a Marine Corps captain.

Hundreds of visitors to the *Hornet* have reported paranormal experiences. These include sightings of apparitions of deckhands and pilots on the flight deck, officers on the bridge, officers wearing "dress whites" in the passageways, men in the medical wing and sick bay wearing khakis or operating room garb, engine room ghosts wearing protective gear that resembled firefighting suits, sailors in blue uniforms, and injured men who appear burned or missing an arm or head.

Sounds have been heard or captured on audio recordings at several locations throughout the ship, including the flight deck, forecastle, hangar deck, engine room, fantail, restrooms, sailors' racks (sleeping quarters), sick bay, and chapel. U.S. Coast Guardsmen, *Hornet* museum staff members, and others who were on board to help restore or maintain the ship have reported hearing disembodied voices offer them advice, bark orders, call for help, and scream as if they are in pain. Lockers, doors, and hatches have been heard opening and closing. Footsteps have been heard on the decks when no one can be seen moving about.

Photographic indications of paranormal activity have been posted on several websites, but the best evidence was shown to me by Jackie Ganiy, president of Sonoma SPIRIT. In the engine room, Jackie and her team captured an infrared image of a man wearing protective gear similar to that worn by firefighters. The image is so detailed that it is easy to see creases in the man's sleeve at his left elbow. On the flight deck, the team captured one of the best orb photographs I've ever seen. The orb floats over the approach end of the flight deck in the vicinity of the aircraft arresting cables. S skull can be seen inside the orb. If this orb represents a spirit presence, it may be the result of a decapitation of a crew member by the arresting cable. Official ship's record indicate that three crew died in this gruesome way.

The *Hornet* is open for self-guided tours, although some parts of the ship may be entered only with a docent. Overnight stays can be arranged.

WALNUT STREET SPIRITS

Between Santa Clara and Clement Avenues

Some streets cross the island of Alameda at its most narrow point of one mile. When they were laid out in the 1850s by the city's earliest residents, they were wide enough for horse-drawn carriages and wagons. But as the city grew and automobiles replaced horses, the streets were not widened. Today, two cars can barely pass each other on Oak, Walnut, Willow, Chestnut and Lafayette Streets. Many of those narrow streets retain Victorian houses. I grew up in one of those Victorians, at 1610 Walnut Street. It was at this house that I had my first paranormal experience.

In the late nineteenth century, several boardinghouses on Lincoln Avenue catered to sailors awaiting departure of their ships. Local historians report that it was common to see several sailors walking Oak, Walnut, and Willow Streets with a sea bag slung over their shoulder as they headed to the estuary docks to board a cargo vessel or fishing boat.

In the 1950s and 1960s, it was still common to see sailors, dock workers, and fishermen walking the narrow streets. One gray morning, while gazing out the front window of my home at skies that threatened rain, I noticed a man walking from my left to right, obviously heading for the docks. As I watched him, I realized that his uniform was not typical of sailors who regularly walked Walnut Street. His uniform, appearing dirty and ragged, seemed old and quite unusual. As I watched him, he turned and looked at me. Instantly, I was stunned, as his eyes appeared as two black sockets. Through a thick beard, he grinned, clearly noticing my startled expression. As he continued walking, he started to fade away. As he passed our driveway, he completely disappeared.

Within seconds, I shook off the shocking image of the man and raced for the door. As I arrived on the sidewalk, I looked in the direction of the estuary, certain that I would see the ragged sailor. I had moved so quickly that the man could not be more than fifty feet from my location, but I could not see him. Walking slightly past our driveway, I continued my surveillance and noticed an odd flash of pale light as the ghostly man crossed Pacific Avenue. I waited for several minutes, hoping that another sailor might appear, but there was nothing else to see. As I walked back to my house, I noticed an isolated pocket of foul odor. The stench was overpowering and reminded me of rain-soaked, rotten clothing or blankets that were occasionally discovered in vacant lots around town.

Weeks later, I confided in my friends, and I was surprised to learn that they had also witnessed ragged sailors walking toward the estuary. Some had also seen the sailors standing on the docks where we fished on Saturday mornings.

The docks along the estuary were replaced by modern structures, but many Victorian homes still stand on the narrow streets. Current residents have reported rarefied images that appear to be men dressed as sailors passing Victorian houses but disappearing as they approached modern structures.

SPIRITS OF THE SHELL MOUND

Mound Street
Between Adams Street and Encinal Avenue

Mound Street in Alameda has always had a reputation as a delightfully strange place. I grew up a few blocks away, and all the kids I knew avoided walking or biking on that street because of rumors that included scary shadows, screams that came out of nowhere, and the sudden disappearance of kids. I assumed most of that was nothing more that misinterpretation of the sound of wind in the trees, screeching of stray cats, and sudden changes in sunlight due to clouds that typically flew over the town on gusty winds. But when I was twelve, I visited the local museum and learned that the street was named for a large Indian mound that was discovered in the 1890s as the city grew. As the docent rambled on, the words "burial mound" caught my attention. It was then that I realized that the weird experiences kids had on that street might be ghosts. About this time, I became friends with kids who lived on Mound Street, and they assured me that several blocks were haunted. Some of them showed me bones and jewelry they found in their backyards while digging. One kid displayed a skull his father had found while digging into the ground to enlarge the basement.

In 1908, archaeologists opened the shell mound and removed the remains of 450 Indians, hundreds of stone implements, shell ornaments, and thousands of shell fragments. The mound measured 400 feet long and 150 feet wide, extended from the present-day Adams Street to Encinal Avenue.

Over the years, I've gathered reports from Mound Street residents who witnessed apparitions of Native Americans appearing in backyards, driveways, and basements. One astonished resident spotted a Native American man standing in his kitchen. These restless souls probably manifest because they are disturbed by the desecration of their graves. Sightings continue on Mound Street because it is likely that not all remains were excavated and reburied elsewhere.

Many ghost hunters, while walking Mound Street late at night, have encountered partial apparitions of Native American spirits and secured audio recordings of words spoken in a language that is unrecognizable.

FORMER SITE OF SPELLBINDING BOOKS

1910 Encinal Avenue

Another popular place visited by supernatural enthusiasts is located on Encinal Avenue, near Lafayette and Chestnut Streets, says Karen Zimmerman. Zimmerman used to own a bookstore in the area, Spellbinding Books, and authored a popular book, *True Hauntings of Alameda*.

"It's near a former train station," said Zimmerman, so there's a lot of history involving movement and expectations there. Although she says she was never hurt by any ghosts or spirits, she was spooked by activity at the spot. "There was activity once when I was on a ladder hanging drapes, for instance," Zimmerman said. "And a rocking chair would move in the night."

Books would fly off the shelves, and signs would mysteriously shift to new spots, she insists. Staff at the bookstore named the rocking chair's spirit "Louisa." Zimmerman hired Ghost Trackers, a South Bay outfit, to investigate the phenomena. "The train used to run nearby," she said, "so maybe there are some ghosts from train accidents."

One bookstore regular who overheard Zimmerman mention trains concurred, describing sounds that she had heard in the basement of the building and the presence of a ghost nicknamed "George."

The former site of this bookstore is now occupied by Blue Dot Café and Coffee Bar.

CROLL'S 1883 RESTAURANT AND BAR

1400 Webster Street
510-748-6075

For more than one hundred years, Croll's Bar was a popular drinking and eating establishment for boxers, sailors, longshoremen, and fishermen residing in Alameda. The place was opened in 1883 with financing provided by Comstock silver baron James Fair. Fair recruited John G. Croll, then manager of the Union Pacific Restaurant in Oakland, to develop the place as prominent feature of the famous Neptune Gardens Amusement Park and Baths (swimming pools), located at the foot of Webster Street in Alameda. Fair allowed Croll to name the place and set up a training resort for boxers. Within months, outdoor exercise areas, practice rings, massage tents, and dining rooms were opened. Boxers and their trainers had priority, but John Croll wisely opened the place to the general public, making it an Alameda landmark business. Several of boxing's greatest fighters trained at Croll's, including Gentleman Jim Corbett (1892–97), John L. Sullivan (1892–95), Ruby Bob Fitzsimmons (1898–99), and Jim Jeffries (1899–1905).

Croll became so successful that he bought the entire establishment from James Fair in 1891, enlarged the facilities, and established stronger business ties with Alameda's Neptune Beach, also known as the Coney Island of the West. All of this came to an end when the great earthquake shook the place on April 18, 1906. Tourism declined to near zero while boxers looked for other, less seismically active places to train and stage fights.

By the late 1920s, Croll's had become a bar that catered almost exclusively to military personnel. Many sailors, soldiers, and marines stationed at the

Croll's Bar and Restaurant has been in business for nearly 150 years.

Alameda Naval Air Station had their last drinks there before shipping out to foreign ports or combat zones of World War II, Korea, and Vietnam. The bar's proximity to the air station and naval harbor made it a first stop for many of the military returning from those historic events. In the 1990s, pool tables and rock bands attracted a younger civilian crowd, but the bar's reputation for trouble spread through the East Bay Area. When I was in high school, my friends and I always avoided passing by the place on a Friday or Saturday night because the riotous atmosphere within often spilled out onto the streets. After I turned twenty-one years old, I patronized the place occasionally, but I always felt unsafe and often got pushed around and soaked with beer.

Over the years, local legends developed about fights, robberies, and shootings that supposedly took place there. There are no official records available confirming fatal shootings, but the eerie atmosphere of the place suggests that something bad happened there.

Croll's Bar closed in 1998 and sat vacant for a few years before reopening in 2005 as an upscale restaurant with garden seating. The laughter, music, and wild banter of the long-deceased drinking crowd can still be heard by those sensitive people who visit the site. These sounds can be detected by psychics and captured on audio recorders late in the evening at the threshold of the Webster Street entrance. They come as brief but unmistakable audible remnants of ghosts that still hang out at the old bar. A dark figure is often seen standing in the doorway looking out into the street. This ghost may be waiting for long-lost friends to return from a war so they can drink a few rounds.

The historic venue is now known as 1400 Bar and Grill.

CHAPTER 2
ALCATRAZ

Sitting 1.5 miles from San Francisco's world-famous Fisherman's Wharf, Alcatraz Island is always included on top ten lists of America's most haunted places. Known for its federal prison and the infamous characters who were incarcerated there, the island has a long history of paranormal activity spanning centuries. Several paranormal research groups have performed investigations of the prison. In September 2009, celebrity ghost hunters Barry and Brad Klinge transported their *Everyday Paranormal* team and vast collection of equipment to the island and performed an extensive investigation that was broadcast on their TV show, *Ghost Lab*. Two months later, an investigative group called Sonoma SPIRIT, led by Jackie Ganiy, was the first to spend an entire night on the island. I joined the cast of the TV show *Ghost Adventures* for a three-day filming on the island in 2013.

The prison's ghosts have been described by Peter James and channeled by world-renowned psychic Sylvia Brown. Ghost hunters Loyd Auerbach, Michael Kouri, and Richard Senate have published detailed reports of their experiences with the ghosts of Alcatraz. With rare exceptions, access to the island is restricted to scheduled tours guided by docents working for the National Park Service.

Named for the huge flocks of pelicans that populated the island and surrounded by dangerous currents, Alcatraz remained undeveloped during the Spanish and Mexican occupation of northern California. Indian legends that told of evil spirits dwelling in caves in the island may have hindered development. After the American annexation of California in 1846, the importance of the island to bay navigation led to the construction of a lighthouse. During the gold rush years (1848–58), a tremendous influx of immigrants and visitations by ships under foreign flags prompted the installation of a military facility on the island. From 1853 to 1858, the U.S. Army Corps of Engineers installed 105 cannons on the island and constructed barracks and other facilities. During the Civil War, the military presence on the island was increased to protect the bay from Confederate sympathizers and privateers sailing outside the Golden Gate. The fort's guns were never fired in battle, but Confederates were imprisoned in the basement of the guardhouse throughout the Civil War.

By 1867, the threat of foreign encroachment had ended, and Alcatraz was converted to a military prison and disciplinary barracks. Inmates were Army deserters and Hopi Indians, but the population remained around 100 until the Spanish-American War of 1898, when as many as 450 prisoners were crowded into tiny cells. After the San Francisco Earthquake of 1906, hundreds of civilian prisoners were incarcerated on the island. A large cell block, the "Citadel," was constructed in 1912 and followed in 1920 by an additional three-story cell block. By 1933, the military had evacuated the island and transferred ownership to the Federal Bureau of Prisons. In August 1934, the first federal prisoners arrived on the island, beginning a twenty-nine-year period that fostered its reputation as an inescapable prison while earning the moniker "the Rock."

Paranormal activity on Alcatraz is the result of Native American spirits, imprints, and hauntings resulting from military and civilian prisoners and numerous sailors, fishermen, and swimmers who lost their lives in the treacherous, swirling currents surrounding the island. At the water's edge, six prisoners were shot and killed during escape attempts. Two others drowned after slipping into the icy water. Hundreds of paranormal imprints of pain and intense emotional experiences were created by prisoners who were tortured in cells called the "strip cells" in D block. In these cells, prisoners were stripped naked and enclosed in total darkness with only a bucket for a toilet and a mattress that was removed during the day. Deprived of contact with others, including the guards, and exposed to very cold temperatures, many prisoners succumbed to the stress and became mentally unstable. One was found inexplicably dead from strangulation later determined not to be self-inflicted.

Several Alcatraz inmates achieved fame before their incarceration. Al Capone (1899–1947) served a little more than four years at Alcatraz before developing symptoms of tertiary syphilis for which he was transferred to

Alcatraz Island was a military prison before federal inmates arrived in 1934.

Terminal Island in Los Angeles. Other notables include George "Machine Gun" Kelly (1895–1954) and his partner, Harvey Bailey (1887–1979); Alvin "Creepy Karpis" Karpowicz (1907–1979); and the leader of the 1946 Alcatraz prisoner revolt, Joseph Cretzer (1911–1946). Others became known because of unique talents developed during imprisonment. Foremost of these was Robert Stroud (1890–1963), also known as the Birdman of Alcatraz. During his incarceration, Stroud became a self-taught expert in ornithology. He was portrayed by actor Burt Lancaster in the movie *The Birdman of Alcatraz*.

Aside from documented prisoner deaths resulting from gunshot wounds inflicted by guards, fatal stabbings during fights among inmates, and drownings that occurred during escape attempts, an unknown number of suicides and natural deaths occurred on Alcatraz that have most certainly added to the spirit population.

Although access to Alcatraz is limited to daylight tours conducted by docents, ghost hunters will have many opportunities to conduct EAP sweeps, snap pictures inside prison cells, and check EMF meters. Ghost seems to be everywhere on Alcatraz, affirming the prison's place on everyone's top ten list of haunted places in America.

Alcatraz Island Ferry departs from Pier 33 in San Francisco. Visitors can contact Ranger Station Information at 415-561-4900. Ferry tickets and reservations can be secured at www.alcatrazislandtickets.com.

GHOSTS OF THE BATTLE OF ALCATRAZ, 1946

On May 2, 1946, the bloodiest event in Alcatraz history took place as a gang of prisoners attempted escape. The event that lasted forty-four hours and took the lives of three convicts and two guards; several other guards were severely wounded. Many inmates refused to participate, but they were so shaken by the seemingly endless barrage of gunfire and explosions that imprints of their frightening experience may be found in several places in cell blocks C and D and in the gun gallery. Two inmates were captured and executed at San Quentin, but imprints of the terror they staged also remain on the prison's "Times Square" and "Seedy Street" corridors.

Bernard Coy (1900–1946) has been identified as the ringleader of the bold escape attempt. Coy arrived at Alcatraz in 1938 with a conviction for bank robbery and a twenty-year sentence. It is likely that soon after his arrival, he heard of the recent escape attempt that ended the life of guard Royal C. Cline and a prisoner who attacked him. This failed escape attempt may have inspired Coy to develop his own plan to flee. By late April 1946, Coy had enlisted trusted inmates Clarence Carnes and Marvin

Alcatraz Federal Penitentiary cells blocks were cold and dark. *Public Domain*

Hubbard. The gang was enlarged with the addition of bank robber Joseph Cretzer, kidnapper and bank robber Sam Shockley, and robber and cop killer Miran Thompson.

The escape started when guard William A. Miller stopped inmate Marvin Hubbard from entering the cell block from the kitchen. While frisking Hubbard, Coy attacked the guard, strangling him with his necktie and beating him nearly unconscious. With stolen keys, Coy and Hubbard opened several cells, releasing others of their gang, while Carnes and Cretzer climbed into the gun gallery and obtained several weapons. Heavily armed, the gang assaulted several guards, forcing them into cells on C block with the intention of using them as hostages to facilitate their escape from the island on the prison boat.

Over the next thirty hours, gunfire was exchanged between guards and inmates several times as the warden attempted negotiations. Finally, late in the evening of May 3, three combat veteran Marine platoons were brought to the island under the joint command of Generals Joe "Vinegar" Stilwell and Frank Merrill. The marines fired into the cell house from several directions and cut holes in the ceiling through which they dropped grenades. The attack was so violent that water pipes in the ceiling broke, flooding the tiers of cell in D and C block. The gunfire and exploding mortar shells were so deafening that several inmates huddled in their cells, certain that the entire building would be reduced to rubble.

As the marine attack continued, guards attempted to enter the cell house gun gallery. Four guards were wounded in this ill-fated attempt to gain a firing position over the inmates in C block, while Harold P. Stites (1897–1946) was mortally wounded by friendly fire. Prison guard Stites was no stranger to prison violence. In 1938, three inmates rushed him while he was on duty in a guard tower. He was forced to shoot two of them, one fatally. His action stopped an escape attempt that ended the life of guard Royal C. Cline (1902–1938).

At 9:40 a.m. on May 4, as marines and armed guards closed in on the rioting inmates, several guards were forced into cells 404 and 403 on C block. When defeat and capture appeared imminent, Cretzer fired into cell 403, wounding several guards and killing guard William A. Miller (1903–1946), who had been injured two days earlier when attacked by Coy in the gun gallery. Lieutenant Joseph H. Simpson, guard Carl "Sunny" Sundstrom, and Captain Henry H. Weinhold were critically wounded by gunshots to the stomach. Prison guard Cecil D. Corwin, guard Ernest B. Lageson Sr., and guard Robert E. Sutter were shot in the face. Prison guard Robert R.

Baker was shot twice in the leg and arm. Prison Guard Joseph Burdette was wounded in the chest.

When the marines finally entered C block, they found the bodies of Bernard Coy (1900–1946), Joseph Cretzer (1911–1946), and Marvin Hubbard (1912–1946) riddled with wounds from bullets and shrapnel from mortars and grenade. Coy was found wearing a guard's uniform, possibly a desperate attempt to escape capture.

For their participation in the Battle for Alcatraz, Miran Thompson (1917–1948) and Sam Shockley (1909–1948) were executed in the gas chamber at San Quentin on December 3, 1948. The youngest member of the gang, Clarence Carnes (1927–1988), was not executed after some of the guards who had been taken hostage reported that he refused to follow Coy's orders to kill them. Carnes received a life sentence but was granted paroled in 1973.

Paranormal experts believe that this tragic event has left intense imprints, and at least two ghosts, in several locations, including D and C block and the gun gallery. At the intersection of the corridor between blocks C and D (called "Seedy Street" by inmates) and the corridor that crosses from the D block door to A block (called "Times Square"), where Coy attacked and seriously injured guard William Miller, there is an intense imprint perceived as thick, cold air in a column that spans the width of two men in contact with each other, as if they were fighting. Empaths perceive fear and anger and retain an impression of a near-death experience sometimes lasting hours after leaving the location.

The most intensely haunted location in cell 403 on C block. In this cell, William Miller was killed, while several others were seriously wounded. Even while standing outside this cell, visitors get that creepy feeling that something tragic happened there. EVP has been captured of shouts and male voices gasping in pain. On one recording, a voice may be heard shouting, "No, no no!" The ghostly image of a guard has been spotted in this cell that may be the spirit of William Miller. The pale image includes bright dots that may be the buttons on the man's uniform.

In several cells on block C, visitors get creepy impressions that may be residuals from the Battle of Alcatraz or the misery of incarceration. My visits to Alcatraz have always included intense paranormal experiences. When *Ghost Adventures* host Zak Bagans and I passed through C on our way to D block, we heard the sound of metal doors slamming shut from high overhead. Park rangers assured us that no one could possibly be on the third tier of C block. A moment later, I perceived the unmistakable sound of an explosion that may be a residual or imprint from the Battle of Alcatraz.

In addition, I have seen the ethereal image of a man standing in cell 403, moaning in pain, and perceived the cold column of air at the site where Coy attacked guard Miller.

It is difficult to perform a paranormal investigation inside the prison. Visitors are closely monitors by docents, and many locations inside the cell house are off limits. Occasionally, local paranormal groups stage an after-hours visit. Contact Bay Area Ghost Hunters, American Paranormal Investigators, Pacific Paranormal Associates, or San Francisco Ghost Society. Alcatraz City Cruises stages behind-the-scenes night tours.

GHOST OF THE BUTCHER

Shower Room, C Block

In the late 1930s, Abie Maldowitz found steady employment with the infamous Murder Incorporated. Founded in 1929 by mobsters Louis "Lepke" Buchalter and Albert "Mad Hatter" Anastasia, this organization was closely aligned with the Jewish mob, Italian American mafia, and notorious crime families of New York. Until its demise in 1941, Murder Incorporated was credited with as many as one thousand murders of criminal rivals, police and FBI informers, and witnesses. Several well-known hit men carried out the organization's contracts, including Tommy "Three-Finger Brown" Lucchese, Martin "Bugsy" Goldstein, Jacob "Gurrah" Shapiro, and Louis Capone. This stable of murderers was joined by Abi "the Butcher" Maldowitz, who allegedly earned his nickname by chopping the bodies of victims into pieces with a meat clever. Little is known about Abi. He is not listed among the most famous hitmen of his time, and his name does not appear on the National Archives at San Francisco website (Former Alcatraz Inmates List), nor can it be found among the prisoner records of the U.S. government (https://www.usa.gov/prisoner-records). Several paranormal investigators, including the celebrated Sylvia Brown, believe that they have encountered his ghost in the shower room of C block.

Thirty years after the prison was closed, caretakers reported inexplicable sounds emanating from the shower room. Sylvia Brown claimed that she was invited to investigate the area by members of the National Park Service who may have believed that a ghostly presence created the sounds of running water, footsteps on a wet floor, and groans. Upon entering the former shower room with former inmate Leon Thompson (no. 1465), Brown reported that she received strong impressions of the remnants of physical violence and the presence of a tall man with beady eyes. Based on her review of person history, she believed that she had encountered the spirit of Abi Maldowitz, who, according the legend, was murdered by two men in the shower room.

Online searches failed to reveal specific information about a murder in the shower room despite the infamy of Maldowitz as a hitman for Murder Incorporated. It is reasonable to expect that rival criminal organizations put a contract on Maldowitz and that at least two Alcatraz inmates carried out the directive. Details of a shower room murder may forever be lost in the fog of history, but the space is incredibly creepy and harbors imprints of terrible events that likely occurred there, including rape.

The shower room is accessed by a stairway at the end of B block that leads to a basement. The open floor plan allowed no privacy, so a murder in this area may have been facilitated by guards who were "distracted" or directly complicit. Many visitors who pass through the shower room feel the heavy presence of negative energy that some have described as fear, pain, awareness of impending death, and anger.

It has been reported that the spirit of the shower room murder also manifests on C Block, perhaps in an effort to gain the attention and protection of guards.

GHOST OF THE BLUDGEONED GUARD

Model Industries Building

The Model Industries Building on Alcatraz sits at the northwest end of Alcatraz Island. Built in 1921, it was used for training military inmates in trades that might enable them to be self-sustaining when their time had been served. The three-story structure contained a blacksmith's shop, plumbing shop, a vocational school, wood shop, and even a band practice room. Early in the federal prison era, it continued to serve as a vocational training facility, but it quickly became apparent that the structure failed to provide architectural features required for high security. Storage rooms and cabinets for tools that might be used as weapons were easily accessed. Many work areas did not provide line-of-sight supervision of inmates. Communication systems were outdated and often failed. Consequently, the vocational program was moved to the New Industries Building in 1939. Tools and equipment in this building were used to manufacture cargo nets for the Navy and anti-submarine nets deployed to keep enemy submarines from entering San Francisco Bay during World War II.

In 1938, the lack of security in the old Model Industries Building became apparent when thirty-six-year-old guard Royal C. Cline (1902–1938) was bludgeoned to death by inmates. Assigned to supervise inmates Thomas Limerick, Rufus Franklin, and James Luces in the woodworking shop, Cline was unarmed and possibly believed that the inmates, preoccupied by their tasks, were unlikely to cause trouble. In a moment of Cline's inattention, the inmates rushed to a window in an escape attempt. Cline attempted to stop the escape but was instead thrown to the floor, where one of the men bludgeoned him with a hammer. Seriously injured, Cline lay on the floor without medical attention for more than an hour as guards rushed to the building to stop the escape attempt. When he was finally transported to the prison hospital, Cline was unconscious for several hours before dying.

The three inmates climbed onto the roof, where they were confronted by guard Harold P. Stites. Thomas Limerick was shot and died on the roof, while Franklin was wounded. The two surviving inmates were tried and convicted of murder and sentence to life imprisonment.

The Model Industries Building has never been open to tourists, and no paranormal investigators have staged ghost hunts there. In 1996, I interviewed the daughter of an Alcatraz guard who recounted stories her father had told her about the ghost in the old building. According to her statements, soon after the escape attempt and Cline's murder, many guards and inmates experienced strange events in the old Model Industries Building. Lights would flicker in the woodworking shop, doors and drawers opened and closed as if moved by unseen hands, and hammers would seemingly disappear only to be found in inexplicable places.

It may seem strange that the ghost of Royal Cline would haunt the place of his horrific death. It is possible that he does not know he is dead. Alternatively, Royal may be waiting for his assailants to return to the scene of the crime so he could exact revenge. Until a paranormal investigation is staged in this building, we cannot be certain that the ghost that caused so much calamity in 1938 is still there. At the very least, imprints of a horrific murder may be discovered.

FORGOTTEN GHOSTS

The Prison Dungeon

Deep under the iconic cell house of Alcatraz is a maze of rooms and hallways seldom seen by tourists, film crews, and even VIP visitors to the island. A remnant of the first prison structure to be constructed on Alcatraz, the stone, cement, and fired bricks capture a moment in time when some of the worst atrocities inflicted on prisoners occurred, leaving durable imprints and some forgotten ghosts.

Captain Joseph Stewart, commander of the Alcatraz military facility in 1859, supervised the development of the island as a military prison initially intended to house soldiers who had committed crimes, including desertion. By 1860, a three-story building had been completed on the island's highest ground that became known as the Citadel. The first floor was placed below ground and surrounded by a dry moat to ensure the integrity of the prison cells. The second and third floors contained barracks for enlisted men, rooms for officers, dining halls, offices, kitchens, and storage rooms for coal and food. Windows featured narrow slits, or embrasures, through which soldiers could fire their rifles if the island were to be attacked. The Citadel was surrounded by an array of heavy artillery and lookout towers to ward off encroachment by the naval power of another nation.

With the outbreak of the Civil War, prisoners of war, including Confederate spies, were incarcerated in the Citadel. The crude cells also housed Americans accused of treason and, by 1873, Native Americans who had been captured during the Indian Wars. By 1868, the island had become better known as a long-term prison instead of a defensive facility to protect San Francisco Bay. The prison population continued to grow throughout the later decades of the nineteenth century, ultimately reaching 450 with the outbreak of the Spanish-American War in 1898. Additions to the prison, needed to alleviate overcrowding, were constructed hastily with wood that led to several problems including fires, escapes, and structural failure. In 1908, after less than fifty years of use, the Citadel collapsed. The rubble was immediately cleared away to make way for construction of the iconic cell house that stands today directly over the former the site of Citadel. The only remaining portion of the old prison is a basement under the cell house that is known as the "dungeon."

Access is through two narrow stairwells—one in D block and another in A block. The duel stairwells were designed with the intention of inflicting psychological stress on prisoners housed in the newer cell blocks. An inmate, sent to solitary confinement, would be seen by A block prisoners as he descended a stair to the dungeon, but his return from the dungeon would not be witnessed as he returned via the stair in D block. In this way, prisoners would assume that no one survived solitary confinement.

The names of prisoners, their crimes, sentences, and dispositions seems to have been lost to history. An exception is the story of Phillip Grosser (1890–1933), a conscientious objector during World War I who was incarcerated on Alcatraz from June 1919 to December 1920. Not known as a cooperative prisoner, Grosser was placed in solitary confinement in the old Citadel cells for several fourteen-day periods. His ordeal was described in detail in a pamphlet he authored titled "Uncle Sam's Devil Island." The horrible conditions included complete darkness; a cold, damp, rat-infested cell; a canvas mat for a bed; a bucket for a toilet; and twice-a-day feedings of bread and water. Not knowing if he would survive the experience, Grosser engraved his name and prisoner number (no. 11461) into a brick still visible in the old Citadel. It seem likely that his stay on Alcatraz had a severely damaging effect on his psyche, as he committed suicide in Boston in October 1933.

There are few reports of ghostly activity in the dungeon. When *Ghost Adventures* filmed an episode there in 2013, the production crew was not allowed to enter the dungeon. A guard I spoke to, on the condition of complete anonymity, told me of several hot spots in the vast array of cells, rooms, and corridors. Odors have been detected that include burning candles, buckets of human waste, intense body odor, and dead rodents. The light of a candle has appeared in several rooms that lasts only seconds. Cells of cold air, approximately the same dimensions as a man, have been encountered in the corridors and at the gun ports. Bursts of sound such as coughing, moans, screams, and gasps of an unseen person with lung disease have been heard by guards and others who enter the dungeon to work on the lighting system.

Warden James. A. Johnston (1874–1954), a nonbeliever, reported an experience that certainly sounds like a valid ghostly encounter. While giving several guests a tour of the prison, the group descended the D cell stairwell to the dungeon. Soon after entering the space, the sound of a woman sobbing was heard by everyone. An inexplicable cold breeze passed through the visitors, but there was no other manifestation. The warden's report indicated that the sound seemed to emanate from inside a dungeon wall. There is no record of female prisons in the dungeon, but one paranormal expert has speculated that the sobbing is an imprint created by the deeply emotional experience of a nurse who entered the cells to care for the prisoners ravaged by confinement under such horrible conditions.

Paranormal experts believe that there may be several ghosts still serving time in the solitary confinement cells of the dungeon. Brief mentions of torture, starvation, and unimaginable psychological stress inflicted by guards also raise suspicion of hundreds of imprints. When the public is finally granted access to the dungeon, it is anticipated that many ghost reports will be posted.

GHOST OF THE CONFEDERATE SOLDIER

Old Warden's House

Long before the prison closed in 1963, ghost stories circulated among the guards and their families. In February 2008, I interviewed a woman who lived on the island for fifteen years, leaving at the age of eighteen. Her father worked as a guard, and her mother performed part-time secretarial work for the warden. Throughout the federal prison's twenty-nine years, guards reported eerie, unexplained screams, metal doors slamming shut, footsteps, cannon fire, gunshots, moans, cries, sobbing, voices whispering, foul odors, and scratching sounds. These unexplained phenomena were encountered throughout the cell blocks and in the laundry, hospital, shops, mess hall, and even the warden's house. Apparitions were also reported. In 1940, guards attending the warden's Christmas party observed a ghostly image appear wearing a gray suit and cap, with mutton chop sideburns. Resembling a Confederate prisoner held on the island during the Civil War, the apparition persisted for several minutes. Moments after it vanished, the room became very cold.

It has been reported that a lady wearing a green dress has been spotted through a window on the first floor of the mansion. Apparently this ghost stands near the gaping hole that was once a shuttered window that opened to a laundry or bathroom. Standing several feet away, witnesses describe her as middle aged with brown hair. It has been suggested that she was the wife of a warden. The stress of living in Alcatraz so close to hundreds of criminals was apparently too much for her. She ended her miserable stay on the island by committing suicide.

Unfortunately, the warden's house now stands in ruins, precluding an investigation of this ghost. Trees and a fence now surround the mansion, but it is possible to view the ruins closely. The three-story mansion must have been an unusual and spectacular sight. Today, its bare walls, open windows, and roofless remains stand against the dense, overcast skies that seems to always hang over the island.

GHOST OF THE BIRDMAN

Alcatraz Infirmary

In the hospital, disembodied sounds of prisoners in agony echo through the rooms. Cries, moans, sobs, and screams are commonly experienced by tourist and docents. Aside from these audio phenomena, sensitive visitors have detected the presence of a kindly man who is eager for conversation. This entity may be Robert Stroud, the "Birdman," who lived in the hospital for eleven years before transferring to the Medical Center for Federal Prisoners in Springfield, Missouri, where he died in 1963. Guards used to play checkers with Stroud, who often carried on long conversations about his studies of birds.

Convicted of murder in 1909, Stroud was incarcerated at McNeil Island Prison in Washington State. Due to repeated threats he made against the guards and other inmates, Stroud was transferred to U.S. Federal Penitentiary in Leavenworth, Kansas, in 1912. He remained there until 1942, when he was transferred to Alcatraz. It was at Leavenworth that Stroud developed his interested in birds, ultimately becoming a recognized expert. He raised more than three hundred canaries and conducted research on the species that served as the basis of two books he authored.

After his transfer to Alcatraz, Stroud's bird studies were limited by prison rules. He became reclusive, eventually spending his final eleven years confined to the prison infirmary. After serving seventeen years at Alcatraz, Stroud's poor health prompted a transfer to a prison medical center in Missouri. There he died on November 21, 1963, at the age of seventy-three.

Robert Stroud's life is depicted in the movie *The Birdman of Alcatraz*, released in 1962. Burt Lancaster portrayed the kindly man who, reputed to have an IQ of 134, befriended birds but killed a man in Alaska in 1909,

The Birdman of Alcatraz, Robert Stroud, still haunts the prison's infirmary. *Public Domain*

stabbed another prisoner in a Washington State prison, attacked a prison hospital orderly, and stabbed a guard to death in a prison cafeteria in 1916.

Is the ghost of Robert Stroud still haunting the prison infirmary? Ghost hunters Sharon and Anne Leong captured video of an unseen spirit moving a trigger object placed adjacent to a tub used by Stroud. Others have reported a solitary bird feather that floats on the still air of Stroud's cell.

Zak Bagans visited the infirmary in 2013 and captured audio recordings of a voice saying "doctor" and another voice screaming followed by "dear God." When two red eyes were spotted in the hospital's hallway, Zak felt drained of energy as a voice said, "Come back."

Paranormal expert and empath Annalisa Bastiani described her experience in the infirmary as depressing since the facility also served as the mental illness ward. When questioned about what spirits occupied the infirmary, a disembodied voice was recorded that stated, "Darkest power."

The infirmary is usually closed to tourist, but guards have often heard sounds as though someone had escaped from a closely manage group tour and wandered into the old cells and operating room. An immediate search always failed to find a living person. Humanoid shadows and apparitions have been spotted in the infirmary, sometimes coinciding with muted cries and screams. One investigator reported a whispered message from a ghost that stated, "I feel good." Psychics, especially empaths, who have visited the area have experienced fear, pain, misery, and a wish to die. Some empaths have found the emotional imprints so overpowering that they had to leave the island.

DEMONS OF D BLOCK

Cells 13 And 14

Cell block D is the site of the most frequent and intense paranormal activity on the island. It was designed to be the "treatment unit" with various degrees of restrictions, isolation, and deprivation. D block prisoners were not allowed to have meals in the mess hall, use the exercise yard, or work in the shops. The boredom and depression they suffered has left audio and emotional imprints in virtually all of the cells of this block.

Six cells in D block were modified as punishment cells. Known as the "strip cells," these cells were used for the most incorrigible prisoners. With only a bucket for a toilet, dim light, and a mattress that was removed from the cell throughout the day, many prisoners in the strip cells went crazy. One of them screamed incessantly throughout most of the night until a bizarre silence filled his cell. In the morning, he was found dead from strangulation with his face frozen in extreme fright.

Visitors who enter the strip cells often experience such frightening impressions that they cannot stay more than a minute. Guards used to tell of beady, evil eyes that appeared in the darkness of empty cells and ghosts of dead prisoners that lined up with the living for roll count in morning.

My first visit to D cells left a deep impression on me. Standing alone in cell 13, the light seemed to grow dimmer as the air temperature fell. Feeling stiff and certain that I could not move, I felt the walls close in and the stale atmosphere start to whirl about me. After several minutes, the air became still, and my attention was draw to the upper corner on the left side of the cell. In that corner, two red beady eyes stared at me. I saw no head or body, no shadow and no change in the dim light that might suggest an apparition. As I stared at the eyes, completely captivated by the red glow, they disappeared, and I felt released by the dense energy inside the cell.

I returned to D block in 2013 with Zak Bagans and the *Ghost Adventures* crew. Upon entering cell 13, Zak immediately experienced some of the same perceptions I had. The red eyes did not appear, but the pulsating walls, dense air, temperatures change, and whirling atmosphere were intense for both of us.

Early the next morning, I left the island with the film crew and began an hour drive home. After thirty minutes of driving, I heard a low-pitched groan that seems to come from the cargo area of my SUV. Initially, I passed it off as the remnants of a thrilling adventure on Alcatraz that penetrated

Detention cells 13 and 14 were investigated by the author and the *Ghost Adventures* TV crew.

my fatigued body. Moments later, the groan became a growl. It wasn't until the next day that I realized that an angry spirit had attached itself to me and was now in my home.

During five days of banishing rituals, I captured an EVP of the spirit's growl that I played for Zak during an interview on his TV show *Aftershocks* (S3, E9). The banishing rituals were successful, and the angry spirit never returned to my home.

Other paranormal investigators have had harrowing experiences in D block cells. Sharon and Anne Leong, highly respected San Francisco–based ghost hunters, toured D block with Zak Bagans and recounted their experiences, which they described as frightening and terrifying. When Zak asked Anne to enter cell 14 with him, she refused, stating that she suspected it was occupied by a demon.

Ghost Adventures crew members Jay and Billy spent several hours in each cell and had experiences similar to mine. The dense air and whirling energy was prominent and seemed to drain the energy from the men. They saw the red eyes they described as dots as a dense veil fell over them. For several minutes, Jay fell into a speechless daze and found it hard to breathe.

No audio was recorded during this investigation, but two photographs captured dense streaks of light interpreted as the manifestations of spirit energy.

OTHER PARANORMAL HOT SPOTS

The Showers: In 1942, Maurice Herring (1908–1942) enter the showers on C block seeking a little private time and soothing hot water. Within minutes, inmate Cecil Snow entered and accosted Maurice. The altercation immediate attracted witnesses, who reported that Herring, being the larger man, threw Snow to the floor and straddled him while repeatedly punching his head. Snow was able to pull a short knife from his pocket and stabbed Herring in the chest and thigh.

Herring left Snow on the floor of the shower and walked a short distance before collapsing. Guards transported Herring to the prison hospital, but without immediate surgical intervention, he died of severe pulmonary hemorrhage.

Despite being the attacker, Snow was acquitted of murder because of witness statements that painted Herring as "hot-tempered," having issued several threats toward Snow and others. Prison staff were stunned by the verdict and directed various disciplinary actions toward Snow. He was "sentenced" to three years of segregation from the prison community that, at times, included complete isolation in the dungeon. When criticized for this action, the warden merely stated that the treatment was "behavior modification."

The showers remain as a hot spot of paranormal activity because of the intense imprint of the Snow-Herring fight and other fatal encounters that occurred there.

The Barbershop: Claude Clyde Colbert Branch took a seat in the prison barbershop with the expectation that he would get cleaned up by a haircut. Apparently, a dispute arose with Ralph Greene, possibly the result of a misunderstanding of who would be next in the barber's chair. Angry and hot-headed, Greene grabbed a metal coat rack and struck Branch in the head. Severely injured but conscious, Branch refused to name the person who assaulted him. It is possible that Branch believed he would survive and thus felt duty-bound to observe the code of the prison community: never interfere with another inmate's game, never help the guards, and never roll over and give up information about another inmate.

Unfortunately for Branch, he lingered two days in the hospital before dying on November 16, 1945. Tragic irony followed as Branch's assailant, Greene, was found not guilty. His defense included allegations that Branch was a homosexual who made unwanted advances toward Greene and others, including attempted rape. Apparently, prison staff were not satisfied with the verdict. They placed Greene in isolation for four and a half years.

THE YARD: The Alcatraz recreation yard is essentially an outdoor pen where inmates were allowed to circulate among themselves, walk the perimeter, play cards, enjoy the little sunshine that permeated the persistent overcast skies, and toss a ball around. Compared to the cramped quarters of a cell, the yard was a much-appreciated opportunity to feel free of the confines of imprisonment. Even with the omnipresent armed guards and tall walls, inmates regarded the yard as their *place* that offered a chance to forget that they were in prison. Most of the friction that took place there between inmates was controlled by the inmates themselves.

On December 4, 1955, however, the general code followed by inmates was violated by prisoner James Bullock. While Bullock played cards with inmate Jimmy Grove and others, Sidney Moore approached and made "threatening gestures." Apparently, Bullock anticipated escalation and pulled a shiv from his pocket, striking him. A shiv is a sharpened object such as a piece of metal or wood absconded from a workshop or other location. Typically, short enough to be easily concealed in a pocket or shoe, the device is usually long enough to hit arteries or major organs. Sidney Moore fell to the ground and bled out, staining the yard with his blood.

THE MORGUE: There is no available inventory of the deceased persons who passed through the prison's morgue before transfer to one of the Bay Area's cemeteries. In the nineteenth century, military personnel who died on the island were kept for a short time in a dedicated room in the infirmary. Upon certification through a death certificate, the deceased was interred at the cemetery on nearby Angel Island unless family members arranged

The morgue of Alcatraz may be the most haunted place on the island.

for burial elsewhere. With the opening of the state-of-the-art morgue in 1910, autopsies could be performed that aided in the identification and prosecution of inmates who murdered staff and prisoners. During the federal penitentiary years, deceased inmates whose remains were unclaimed by relatives were sent to the country coroner, who placed them in an unmarked pauper's grave.

Located on the northwestern side of the island, between the water tower and retaining wall of the yard, the small facility had thick walls to aid in the preservation of dead bodies and gunpowder, if the need were to arise. Three vaults surrounded an examination table that still stands in the space, covered with moss. A skylight in the ceiling was installed, but it failed to properly illuminate the morgue.

There have been no paranormal investigations of the morgue, but there is high suspicion that the place is haunted by several spirits.

CHAPTER 3

YERBA BUENA AND TREASURE ISLANDS

In 1775, Captain Juan Manuel de Ayala sailed his ship, the *San Carlos*, into San Francisco Bay and anchored near a tiny island covered by pelicans. His crew called the place *Isla de Alcatraces* ("Island of the Pelicans"), which persisted until 1826, when English Captain Frederick Beechey arrived. Surveying the bay's landmarks, he gave the name Alcatraz to the island that later served as a federal penitentiary and called Ayala's island Yerba Buena ("Good Grass") after the settlement that would later become the city of San Francisco. Apparently, many agreed that the name was appropriate because a fragrant plant was abundant on the island that tasted like spearmint.

During the gold rush, hundreds of goats were grazed on the island, prompting locals to call the place Goat Island. Other names were applied to the island such as Wood Island and Bird Island, but in 1931, the U.S. Board on Geographic Names declared its official name to be Yerba Buena Island.

For decades, the island was used only for grazing goats, fishing, and gathering firewood, until the U.S. military recognized its importance in protecting San Francisco Bay from intrusion by foreign powers during the Civil War. From 1870 to 1996, the island was developed as a military installation, including a row of mansions for admirals and a lighthouse. In 1933, Yerba Buena Island was included as a vital support point for construction of the Oakland–San Francisco Bay Bridge.

The military value of the tiny island was greatly expanded with the construction of Treasure Island in 1936. Considered an appendage of Yerba Buena due to a causeway connecting the two islands, Treasure Island was constructed by dredging bay mud and sand and filling the shoals of

Yerba Buena Island, creating an additional four hundred acres of land that was later covered with fifty thousand cubic yards of topsoil. The name for this new island was selected because of the widespread belief that the mud and sand of San Francisco Bay used to create the land mass contained tons of gold washed down from the sierras over several millennia.

Yerba Bena Island is an anchor for the Oakland–San Francisco Bay Bridge. *Public Domain*

During World War II, the U.S. Navy seized both islands from the city of San Francisco and established the headquarters of the Twelfth Naval District. Docks, warehouses, barracks, runways, and hangars were constructed to facilitate dispersal of men and supplies throughout the Pacific and repair of ships and airplanes. An enclave on Yerba Buena Island became the residence of the commander in chief of the U.S. Pacific Fleet (CINCPACFLT), Chester A. Nimitz.

NAVSTA Treasure Island had a Naval Auxiliary Air Facility in order to support helicopters, fixed-wing planes, seaplanes, blimps, dirigibles and airships, and a U.S. Navy/USMC electronics school. During World War II, more than twelve thousand men per day were processed here for Pacific assignments, and thousands more were processed for separation in the aftermath of the war. The psychiatric ward of the naval base at Treasure Island was used to study and experiment on naval sailors who were being discharged for being homosexual.

Several movies and TV shows have been filmed at Treasure Island's old hangars (Building 3 and Building 4), including *The Matrix*, *Rent*, *The Pursuit of Happyness*, and *Indiana Jones and the Last Crusade*. The popular TV show *Nash Bridges* was filmed there from 1996 to 2001. Building 180 (warehouse) and Building 111 (former firehouse) served as film settings for the NBC series *Trauma*. In 2018, the Treasure Island Museum building served as a mental hospital setting for the Netflix series *The OA*. *MythBusters* also regularly shot footage of its various experiments on the island.

Today, both Treasure Island and Yerba Buena Island are accessible to the public for hiking, cycling, sailing, fishing, and exploring several historic buildings that date from the island's early military period and the 1939 Golden Gate International Exposition.

FORMER U.S. NAVAL HEADQUARTERS

1 Avenue of the Palms
Treasure Island
San Francisco

From February 18, 1939, to September 29, 1940, San Francisco hosted the Golden Gate International Exposition, attracting 17 million visitors from around the world to Treasure Island. Showcasing the accomplishments and productivity of many nations bordering the Pacific Ocean, the huge park included several massive exhibition halls, fountains, light displays, and an eighty-foot-tall statue of the goddess of the Pacific Ocean, Pacifica. Today, few remnants of this spectacular event remain on Treasure Island. The most impressive structure is the former Pan American Airways terminal, which became a U.S. Navy station and headquarters of the Pacific Fleet.

Completed in 1938, the building first served as the terminal for Pan American Airways, which offered seaplane service to and from destinations throughout the Pacific. Many visitors from countries bordering the Pacific Ocean used the airline for travel to the Golden Gate International Exposition.

When the exposition closed in 1940, San Francisco intended to use the island as an international airport and continue Pan American's "China clipper" service, which had started in 1935 in Alameda. Envisioning flying boat service to destinations throughout the Pacific and Central America, civic leaders recognized that Clipper Cove offered calms waters for navigating the giant seaplanes and that the exhibition halls could be upgraded and continue to serve as hangars. Before these plans could be enacted, World War II broke out; the U.S. Navy—well aware of the strategic importance of a large island that could service ships, provide training facilities, and accommodate amphibious aircraft—seized the land.

The Navy created a massive base comprising barracks for twelve thousand sailors and marines, a hospital with more than one thousand beds, an electronics and radio communications training school, and several other buildings, docks, and piers to support the Navy's activity as a major departure and receiving point for military personnel who embarked on aboard surface ships and submarines. Air operations expanded rapidly after the Navy took over Treasure Island. An airfield that served as a base for blimps and land-based aircraft was constructed, and seaplane ramps were widened. All of these renovations and additions were managed by naval

The former Pan American Airways terminal served as U.S. Navy headquarters in World War II.

officers working in the old Pan American Airways building that was now designated Headquarters, U.S. Naval Station Treasure Island.

For decades, local paranormal investigators have speculated that the administration building harbors hundreds of imprints and at least one ghost. Imprints may be residuals from millions of travelers who arrived at Treasure Island for the Golden Gate Exposition and military personnel facing the horrors of World War II that awaited them in the western Pacific. In the grand foyer that now houses the museum, sensitives frequently perceive cold spots and the movement of air as if a crowd were rushing past them. Some sensitives report the perception of sound bursts of footsteps and indistinct audio phenomenon described as a "noisy crowd."

A somewhat confidential report has been passed around some local paranormal investigators of an apparition of a sailor that appears in the old Pan American control tower stairway. There is suspicion that this fellow fell on the stairs and died sometime during World War II. This location has not been accessible to ghost hunters, but a painter who worked on restoration of the building reported seeing the apparition twice. He also reported the sound of footsteps at a time when no other living person was in the building. There may be several other ghosts in this historic building. Museums tend to be gathering points for spirits that may have died elsewhere but were attracted to the ambience or theme of a specific venue or authentic relics that were significant in their lives. A good example is the USS *Hornet* in Alameda. Many spirits on board that warship died elsewhere but find refuge in a World War II aircraft carrier, including a friend of mine who died in Vietnam.

In 1975, the old administration building was opened to the public as the Treasure Island Museum, with exhibits honoring the Navy and Marine

Corps from 1800 to the present. The museum closed in 1997 as the Navy withdrew from the island. After sitting vacant for many years, the museum reopened in 2008. Among its many attractions is a spectacular mural by photorealist artist Lowell Nesbitt (1933–1963), measuring 251 feet long and 26 feet high representing scenes in the history of the Navy and Marine Corps in the Pacific since 1813. Completed in 1976 to commemorate the opening of the museum, it stood over hundreds of artifacts from the Golden Gate Exposition, military operations in the Pacific, and the China clipper seaplane service.

For access to the museum, contact TreasureIslandMuseum.org/tours or call 415-413-8462.

QUARTERS 1

The Nimitz House
1 Whiting Way
Yerba Buena Island

The Nimitz House on Yerba Buena was constructed in 1900 and designated "Quarters 1" to indicate that it would serve as the private residence of a U.S. Navy admiral. Its first occupant was Rear Admiral Henry Glass (1844–1908). In the ensuing years, several flag officers called the place home, including Vice-Admiral John W. Greenslade (1880–1950), a veteran of the Spanish-American War, the Philippine Insurrection, the Cuban Pacification Campaign, and both world wars; Rear Admiral Robert W. Cary (1890–1967), holder of the Congressional Medal of Honor and wartime skipper of the USS *Savannah* and USS *Brooklyn* during the invasion operations at Sicily, Salerno, and Anzio; and Rear Admiral Hugo N. Osterhaus, USN (1851–1927), who started his naval career in 1900 and served in World War I as commander of one of the first transports to carry American troops to France. Its most distinguished resident, however, was Fleet Admiral Chester W. Nimitz (1885–1966), who served as commander in chief of the U.S. Pacific Fleet and the Pacific Ocean Areas, commanding Allied air, land, and sea forces during World War II. The list of occupants is long, but Nimitz stands out as the only admiral to die in the house.

The presence of these heroic men in the grand mansion with their devoted families and an endless stream of visitors, including other high-ranking military officers and foreign dignitaries, has most certainly created intense and durable imprints. It is also likely that some of those who lived in the house but died elsewhere may have returned as ghosts to relive great moments in history, including the start of World War II in 1941, support for naval battles in the Pacific, and the surrender of Japan in 1945. So it isn't any wonder that local ghost hunters have tagged Quarters 1 as a prime target for paranormal investigation despite being closed to the public. Today, visitors may view the mansion's exterior and perhaps peek through its windows, but access is tightly controlled by the Treasure Island Museum Association and the National Park Service.

At the conclusion of World War II, Nimitz was relieved of his fleet command and became chief of naval operations. He faced the arduous task of reducing the most powerful navy in the world from a combat-ready force to a peacetime military while fostering the transition into the modern-age of jet aircraft and nuclear-powered submarines. It has been said that Nimitz's greatest accomplishment as CNO was his strong support of Admiral Hyman Rickover's effort to covert the U.S. submarine fleet to nuclear propulsion.

Nimitz officially retired in December 1947, but his rank as fleet admiral was a lifetime designation that included full benefits and pay. He and his wife, Catherine, resided in Berkeley, California, until 1964, when he was seriously injured by a fall. Looking across the bay to Yerba Buena, the admiral must have realized that his final years should be spent on a naval base. Soon after he and Catherine moved to Quarters 1, the admiral suffered a stroke complicated by pneumonia. After a brief stay at the U.S. Naval Hospital in Oakland, he returned to the island only to die on February 20, 1966, four days shy of his eighty-first birthday.

If the Nimitz House is haunted, it is most likely the spirit of Admiral Chester Nimitz that gives visitors and people working in the mansion that curious feeling that some unseen person is standing nearby. Nearly sixty years of devotion to country and service in the Navy would most certainly culminate in a finely focused energy that would not dissipate after bodily death. The view from Quarters 1 would afford the ethereal admiral a view of the huge Alameda Naval Air Station and the giant nuclear-powered aircraft carriers that frequented the base during the Vietnam War.

Reports of intriguing experiences that may be encounters with the paranormal have been passed to me through sources that were often not primary. Various people who have worked in the mansion—including painters,

The Yerba Buena Island mansion where Fleet Admiral Chester Nimitz died in 1966.

plumbers, cleaners, and more—have mentioned bizarre experiences such as movement of tools, doors that moved, the sound of footsteps, the sound of rattling glassware, and bursts of human vocalization. Investigation of these phenomena may be staged only with the permission of the Treasure Island Museum Association and the National Park Service. The house is slowly fading from its once glorious past. The white paint is faded and marred by exhaust from traffic on the Bay Bridge.

An excellent video tour of the house, hosted by one of its former residents, Rear Admiral John Bitoff, may be found on YouTube.

GHOST OF THE DEDICATED LIGHT KEEPER

Yerba Buena Lighthouse

Lighthouses are often regarded as haunted places where a paranormal experience is highly probable. There is something about the desolate location at the edge of a ragged coast lashed by raging seas that conjures notions of a secret history that may include shipwrecks that killed sailors and passengers, accidental death by falling from a great height, or depressed light keepers who resorted to suicide. I've investigated several lighthouses, from Seattle's Puget Sound to San Diego, and found astonishing imprints in all of them and apparitions of ghosts that cannot give up the duty guarding ships from disaster. The lighthouse on Yerba Buena Island serves as a beacon for ships navigating the relatively calm waters of San Francisco Bay, but local paranormal investigations have speculated that the place likely harbors at least one ghost whose life history suggests an intense devotion to duty that death could not dissolve.

Constructed in 1875, the Yerba Buena lighthouse stands twenty-five feet on ground fifty feet above the high-water line. The keeper's residence, constructed in the same year but significantly enlarged in 1897, was placed about eighty yards away, on a slope above the lighthouse. Over the first eighty-five years of operation, the light was managed by seventeen keepers with periods of duty ranging from one year (James C. Moore, 1946–47) to the longest hitch of seventeen years (Herbert H. Luff, 1904–21). One who stands out with a fascinating history that may point to a haunting was John P. Kofod (1858–1933), who served as light keeper from 1921 to 1928. John served as assistant light keeper from 1903 to 1914, when he transferred to the lighthouse on East Brother Island passage into San Pablo Bay. He returned to Yerba Buena in 1921 as principle keeper until his retirement in 1928.

John's only daughter, Anna (1887–1969), was born in the light keeper's residence at Point Sur and spent all of her childhood and early adult life at West Coast lighthouses. While residing on Yerba Buena Island, she met and married Nathaniel Fanning in 1908, a Navy radio operator stationed on the island. On July 17, 1909, while living in the keeper's house, Nathaniel nearly destroyed the place when his illicit collection of radio gear sparked and set the second floor on fire. Cruising nearby, the Navy tug *Vigilant* sounded the fire alarm and pumped water from the bay to douse the flames.

If there is a ghost in the old keeper's house, it is likely that of John Kofod. After a lifetime of service to the U.S. Lighthouse Service that included eighteen years at his favorite station, it seems plausible that he would return to the place where his only child grew up and married, a place with a peaceful ambience that offered a view of a spectacular city. Another likely ghost is that of Walter Fanning (1908–2008), grandson of John Kofod. Walter had a lifelong love of lighthouses. Upon his death, his daughter, Susan Montague, said, "East Brother and Yerba Buena islands were the loves of his life. He loved the history of the islands. They were very dear to his heart."

Walter was born in the keeper's house on Yerba Buena and followed in the footsteps of his grandfather by becoming the keeper of the East Brother Island lighthouse. Lifelong devotion to a unique profession, dedication to a family tradition, a somewhat romantic view of the lifestyle of keeper families, and a love of the history of lighthouses would most certainly entice a ghost to resume residence in a place such as the Yerba Buena lighthouse.

There are no reports of paranormal activity in the keeper's house, which since 1958 has served as the official residence of the admiral in command of the U.S. Coast Guard sector San Francisco. If a ghost haunts the lighthouse or the residence, any record of paranormal activity will not be disclosed to the public.

NAVAL STATION TREASURE ISLAND

The Old Hangars
Buildings 2 and 3

Completed in June 1938, Buildings 2 and 3 were designed to serve as hangars for Pan American Airways seaplanes that flew throughout the western Pacific, serving major cities in China and the Philippines and the islands of Oahu, Midway, and Wake. With doors spanning two hundred feet and a ceiling of sixty-five feet at the center, the huge buildings could accommodate two seaplane simultaneously, allowing crews to carry out maintenance and repair while sheltered from cold and damp weather. Originally intended to be a part of San Francisco's international airport, which included a runway on Treasure Island for land-based aircraft, the buildings were repurposed for the 1939 Golden Gate International Exposition as exhibit halls.

The aircraft hangars housed the famous "China clipper" seaplanes use by Pan American Airways.

Building 3, offering 48,600 square feet of floor space, served as the Palace of Fine and Decorative Art. Its walls were covered with plaster to create a more formal appearance, while the entrance was adorned with plaster scallops and flutes. The building housed a collection of art valued at $20 million that was curated by Dorothy Wright Liebes (1897–1972) and Shepard Vogelsang (1901–1969). Liebes was an American textile designer and weaver renowned for her innovative, custom-designed modern fabrics for architects, interior designers, and fashion designers. She was known as the "mother of modern weaving." Shepard Vogelsang was a designer and decorative artist.

Building 2 was upgraded to appear like a modern art gallery with the addition of a plaster sculpture of the goddess Pacifica over the main entrance. Dubbed the Palace of Transportation, the hall housed examples of the earliest automobiles dating from the 1890s and mockups of future cars including amphibious vehicles, watercraft, and airplanes.

After the internal exposition, the City of San Francisco intended to resume its plan of establishing an international airport on Treasure Island, with seaplane and land-based air travel service, but the island and all of its buildings were seized by the Navy and renovated for military use. From 1941 to 1997, the intensity of human energy contained within the old hangars was undoubtedly extreme. There is no accessible record of accidents, injuries, or deaths in the hangars during the Navy's occupancy, but the urgency of wartime activity experienced by hundreds if not thousands of aircraft workers and crews most certainly created imprints that are quite durable. Today, space within the hangars is leased to various businesses including food and vine vendors, recreational facilities, and movie and TV production companies. No malevolent paranormal experiences have been reported by workers or patrons, but sensitives who visit the old hangars have reported energy anomalies that include cold spots, explained air movement, sound bursts, brief visions of shadows or humanoid shapes, and inexplicable changes in mood including depression and anxiety. A formal paranormal investigation of either hangar has never been performed, but local ghost hunters suspect that both buildings contained hundreds of imprints.

The most fascinating mystery associated with Building 2 is the disappearance of the two-man crew of the "ghost blimp." The U.S. Navy L-class airship, a dirigible, took off from Treasure Island at 11:15 a.m. on August 16, 1942, for a routine anti-submarine patrol off the coast of San Francisco. During several hours of flight, no radio transmissions were received from the airship with the exception one message indicating that the

The cabin of Navy blimp L-8, which crashed in Daly City without a crew on board. *Public Domain*

mission was proceeding without incident. Late in the afternoon, the airship appeared over Ocean Beach, made brief contact with the ground, and then proceeded into the city, eventually crashing at 419 Bellevue Avenue in Daly City. People in the neighborhood rushed to the crash site only to find the crew missing.

Examination of the wreckage revealed no evidence of enemy fire or blood that might explain the lack of crew, which included Lieutenant Ernest DeWitt Cody (1914–1942) and Ensign Charles Ellis Adams (1908–1942). Reportedly, parachutes were not removed from their lockers, and the airship's radios were in working order. During a lengthy investigation, a few observations were recorded that did little but enhance speculation that something other than an operation failure caused the crash and disappearance of the crew. One woman on Ocean Beach reported that she saw *three* men in the blimp as it approached the coast. Another reported seeing parachutes. A Pam Am captain reported the blimp flying at two thousand feet, far above its usual operating altitude. Witnesses in Daly City reported that the blimp appeared damaged and described it as a "big broken wiener." Further speculation arose suggesting that the men had defected to a Japanese submarine, were murdered by a stowaway, fell overboard while fighting about a woman, or were abducted by aliens. More recently, paranormal researchers have speculated that some malevolent energy on Treasure Island may have boarded the blimp with the crew and threw them overboard.

Recently, aviation disaster investigators have offered a more plausible explanation. They suggest that one of the crew exited the cabin to repair something on the exterior of the airship. When the man lost his footing, the second pilot attempted to save him but both fell into the sea. The Navy has accepted this as the most plausible explanation without citing what exterior object might have need repair. The mystery remains so compelling that the control cabin of the airship remains on display at the National Naval Aviation Museum in Pensacola, Florida.

GRAVES OF THE ISLAND SETTLERS

Yerba Buena Cemetery

Soon after the discovery of gold in California in 1848 and the massive influx of miners, sailors, ranchers, bankers, and gamblers in 1849, new arrivers in San Francisco quickly became enamored of Yerba Buena Island. One of the first settlers was Captain Edward Lindsey (1813–1852), who arrived in 1850 with his wife and six children. The place was close enough to the city to facilitate the acquisition food and building supplies yet an adequate distance from the raucous Barbary Coast, which hosted hundreds of bars and brothels. The earliest settlers on the island quickly establish two essentials: a house that could withstand the cold, wet weather and a cemetery.

The Yerba Buena Cemetery opened in 1849 with the internment of Peter and John Black, who had served as seamen aboard the USS *Ewing*. On September 13, 1849, while rowing Midshipman William Gibson from the ship to a San Francisco pier, the brothers attacked Gibson and threw him overboard. With three accomplices, the brothers escaped up the Sacramento River, where they were apprehended. The five sailors were convicted of mutiny and desertion. John Black was also charged with attempted murder. On October 29, 1849, John was hanged from the yardarm of the USS *Ewing*, while his brother, Peter, was hanged from the mast of the USS *Savannah*. Despite their convictions, the brothers were buried at the Yerba Buena settlement's cemetery.

In the 1850s, the cemetery filled quickly. Captain Edward Lindsey and his son Edward Lacklin Lindsey (1848–1855) became early occupants of graves together with several military officers and members of their families, including children. Initially, graves were marked with wood plaques, but it quickly became apparent that the bay's weather caused names and dates to deteriorate quickly. The Army ordered granite markers, but they arrived on the island after most of the old wooden markers had rotted or been removed.

Fortunately, a cemetery map was found in Washington, D.C., and markers were placed over the correct graves.

The cemetery was closed in 1938 when organizers of the 1939 World's Fair, to be staged on Treasure Island, realized that visitors would have to pass by the "distressing" cemetery on the approach to the fair's entrance. Contractors were immediately set to work removing the graves to the San Francisco National Cemetery at the Presidio.

Many paranormal experts believe that several bodies remain in the old cemetery plot because grave removal contractors often failed to do a thorough job. At the start of the twentieth century, San Francisco had thirty-eight cemeteries. With the onset of the bubonic plague in 1902 and pressures from real estate developers, city leaders ordered all graves to be removed to a site at Colma, south of the city, except those in the national cemetery at the Presidio, the Neptune Columbarium, and the old Mission Dolores. Faced with the challenge of removing thousands of graves, contractors often just removed headstones and left many bodies in place, six feet underground. It is likely that a similar work ethic influenced the removal of graves from Yerba Buena Cemetery. Paranormal investigators have found electromagnetic anomalies at this site. Dowsing rods also signal anomalies interpreted as interred bodies.

There is some mention in Yerba Buena histories of a cemetery dedicated solely to military personnel located on Yerba Buena Road, at a site now occupied by the dog park.

STRANGE GRAVES

Yerba Buena Island

Historians and archaeologists agree that Yerba Buena Island is littered with graves. Aside from the official cemeteries discussed in other sections of this chapter, unmarked the graves of humans and animals have been uncovered in several places. The energy of the older burial locations has certainly dissipated over the passage of hundreds of years or more, yet sensitive people often detect electromagnetic anomalies in well-defined, specific locations that may arise from a border between organic and inorganic material. The electromagnetic anomalies may be detected with dowsing rods with much greater specificity than E-M meters typically used by ghost hunters.

During the dredging of bay mud and sand to create Treasure Island, the remains of a prehistoric mammoth were uncovered. The largest remnant was a tusk nine feet long that was carbon-dated to 250,000 years ago. The discovery was verified by Professor Vertress Lawrence VanderHoof, professor of geology at University of California–Berkeley and member of the Manhattan Project team that developed the atomic bomb. The discovery site is believed to be Clipper Cove. Currently, explorers comb the shore of Clipper Cove with sharp eyes and metal detectors where shark teeth are often found.

Another animal grave of much more recent vintage can be found near Quarters 1 on the east side of Yerba Buena Island. A horse named Matilda is buried under a concreate slab, and despite the popularity of this horse with the military garrison on the island in 1900, there is no headstone or monument.

According to reports of soldiers stationed on the island, Matilda was a high-energy horse known for kicking the blacksmith who tried to shoe her. When she pulled the commandant's Victorian carriage, "Mathilda sensed the importance of the moment and, though somewhat spavined, she would make the trip with a great show of spirit. Her response to the crack of the coachman's whip was instantaneous," as noted by Marcia Edwards Boyes in her book of collected stories, *The Legend of Yerba Buena Island.*

It has been reported that before the body was covered, several officers and enlisted men passed by the grave and dropped into it personal objects as a demonstration of affection and respect for Matilda. One soldier dropped his good conduct medal into the grave, something highly valued by military personnel.

In the 1860s, fishermen and goat herders discovered the remnants of an Indian village in a location now occupied by the Coast Guard Base. Archaeological investigation in the nineteenth century was crude at best, but records indicate that a large village established by the Tuchayunes tribe once stood on the east side of Yerba Buena Island, under the eastbound lanes of the bridge, midway between the torpedo assembly building and the Coast Guard's buoy maintenance facility. Ruins of dwellings were found together with huge piles of shells and bones. Pits used for cremation of the deceased were also uncovered, some still filled with ashes and human bones.

A report dated January 21, 1899, describes a discovery made by a laborer as he dug a pit four feet deep near the summit of the island. Scientists from University of California–Berkeley were called to the scene. They unearthed the skeleton of a man who once stood seventy-eight inches tall, much taller than Indians of the time. During construction of the Oakland–San Francisco Bay bridge tunnel, more unmarked graves were discovered, some in a sitting position. Aside from bones, these burial holes also contained stone mortars, pots, and the skeleton of a dog.

At the summit of the island—344 feet above the low-water mark—a unique grave was dug by an Italian immigrant in the 1850s. With a strong desire to commit suicide and ensure that his body would be properly buried, he created a mechanism that would fill the grave with soil when triggered by the sound of his pistol as he fired a bullet into his head. The suicide was a success, but the grave was only partially filled. Days later, his unfilled grave was discovered. Policed removed the body and reburied it in a pauper's grave in San Francisco.

Apparently, the grave and its location became legendary and attracted the attention of a suicidal alcoholic man. This fellow could not dig his own grave, so he decided to use the empty hole at the island's summit. His suicide plan failed because he drank a large quantity of whiskey, possibly to lessen the pain of a bullet entering his brain, but the beverage caused him to fall asleep. When the sleeping drunk was discovered by soldiers, he was transported to San Francisco and held in jail until he regained sobriety. The location of this "suicide" grave is about thirty feet south of the island's highest point marker stone.

Historians and archaeologists have documented four additional unmarked graves on Yerba Buena. In 1860, Daniel Dowling was swept overboard from a stone scow, or barge, as the vessel was slammed against the rocks of Yerba Buena. Daniel was buried near the island's summit, which is now designated Hilltop Park. At this location, Captain Edward Lindsey and his son Edward Lacklin Lindsey were buried and marked by a headstone. It has been reported that these graves were moved to the island's principle cemetery sometime in the 1860s and removed to a final resting spot at San Francisco National Cemetery in 1938.

At Hilltop Park, historians believe an unmarked grave exists that contains the remains of a sailor who fell from the rigging of the ship *Melancthon*. At nearby Panorama Park, island legend states that the wife of an army officer was buried at a location that would provide her with a view of the sunset through the Golden Gate. Apparently, while alive, this was a favored a location that offered solace from the grief she experience when her husband's affair was discovered.

Paranormal investigators have discovered specific locations at Hilltop Park and Panorama Park that trigger dowsing rod reactions and instruments that detect anomalies in the electromagnetic field. These specific locations, covering no more than a few square feet, are believed to be unmarked graves.

GHOSTS OF THE HAUNTED BRIDGE

The Oakland–San Francisco Bay bridge tunnel through Yerba Buena Island was started in 1934 and completed in 1936. The single-bore, two-level tunnel was, at the time, considered the world's largest bore tunnel. The upper deck served automobile traffic, while the lower deck was reserved for trucks and the Key System trains. Train crossings were discontinued in 1958, and the lower level was opened to eastbound traffic, while westbound drivers enjoyed the view from the upper level. Unlike the neighboring Gold Gate Bridge, this bridge was never a most favored venue for people seeking to commit suicide. Records are not easily accessed, but reports indicate that fewer than 100 people have jumped from this bridge, in contrast to the 1600 known suicides from the Golden Gate Bridge.

Much of the ghostly activity experienced on the Bay Bridge is the result of traffic accidents. Drivers traversing the Yerba Buena tunnel and entering or leaving the tunnel have reported some amazing experiences that include sighting apparitions, knocking on windows by unseen hands, sudden cold air filling the car, unexplained lights glowing on the tunnel walls, and the sound of screeching tires despite the smooth flow of traffic.

On the eastern span of the bridge, the ghost of a young woman has been spotted by several drivers. This ghost is believed to be a victim of the 1989 Loma Prieta earthquake, which caused a fifty-foot section of the upper deck to collapse onto the lower deck. The collapsed roadway caused hundreds of drivers to be stalled on both decks. In an effort to unravel the traffic, emergency workers directed some cars in the wrong direction, eastward toward the collapsed section of the bridge. Twenty-three-year-old Anamafi Moala trusted the directions she had been given and drove her car into the gap, killing herself and seriously injuring her brother. At the location of this tragedy, drivers have reported a transparent apparition appearing in their rear seat. Officially, only one death is attributed to the bridge collapse, but the ghost of a headless man, running next to a car, has been seen in the location of Moala's death.

As the upper roadway emerges from the Yerba Buena tunnel, the ghost of a man in a trench coat and fedora hat has been seen as he walks toward San Francisco. It is believe that this is the ghost of a driver whose car ran out of gas in 1948. As this unfortunate fellow walked the emergency phone located on the bridge, he was struck by a car and killed.

Another tragic accident that occurred on February 15, 2024, may be linked strong impressions perceived by sensitives and empaths at the Treasure

Island exit from eastbound lanes. At this site, two people were killed instantly while a third person was fatally injured after their Mini Cooper stalled on the bridge. California Highway Patrol reported that the stalled vehicle was hit from behind by a Tacoma truck. When passing through this specific location, empaths perceive abrupt fear and pain. One empath reported to me that when driving through this location on several occasions, she has experienced an intense sensation of being crushed that lasts no more than a few seconds.

Aside from these and other accidents that may have created ghosts and intense imprints on the Bay Bridge, the spirits of some of the twenty-nine men who died during its construction may still be on the job. In 1933, Harry Hill, William Marotzke, B.S. Hill, and Lloyd Evans were the first to die. Eleven men died together in 1935 when their safety net tore. Safety nets saved the lives of nineteen men who fell from their workplaces. They became known as members of the "Half-Way to Hell Club." Ray Randall and Louis Knight were the last to die in 1937. A plaque that once stood at 415 Fifth Street in San Francisco honored those men, but it was removed due to encroachment by urban campers.

CHAPTER 4
ANGEL ISLAND

On August 5, 1775, the Spanish ship *San Carlos*, under the command of Juan de Ayala (1745–1797), sailed into San Francisco Bay and paid homage to an island for a safe anchorage by naming the place Isla de Nuestra Senora de Los Ángeles ("Island of Our Lady of the Angels"). Cutting down many of the trees, the Spanish gathered wood for the ship's stoves and hunted deer that historians believe swam across a narrow straight from the mainland. In 1841, the island became known to East Coast Americans when Richard Henry Dana published his account of visiting San Francisco Bay in 1836 while serving aboard the U.S. merchant ship *Pilgrim*. Dana noted that the island had no development of any kind, but charts of the day designated his anchorage as Ayala Cove, while local Mexicans referred to the island as "Wood Island."

With the American acquisition of California in 1846, new charts of the bay were created, including one made by Cadwalader Ringgold that officially designated Wood Island as Island de Los Angeles. Considered an essential element in the protection of the bay from invasion by foreign navies, military occupation of the island started immediately, with quarry operations to obtain stone for construction of fortifications and gun emplacements on both Angel and Alcatraz Islands, as well as Fort Point in San Francisco.

During the American Civil War, fear of naval attack by Confederate ships prompted enhanced militarization of the island with the establishment of Camp Reynolds, garrisoned by the Third Artillery Regiment under command of Lieutenant John L. Tiernon (1841–1910). By 1864, Camp

Reynolds housed five hundred soldiers and their families and maintained thirteen heavy cannons. Several buildings that composed this fort still stand surround the parade ground at the western end of the island.

Construction of Fort McDowell, on the eastern side of the island, began in the 1890s and continued through World War II. Initially planned as a processing center for soldiers destined for the Spanish-American War (1898) in the Philippines, the installation also included a detention camp. In the five years following the war, nearly 90,000 soldiers passed through the camp before discharge from service. Large numbers of returnees from overseas suffered from contagious diseases, including smallpox, prompting the Army to construct large hospital and isolation facilities. During World War I and World War II, the fort was expanded to accommodate as many as 4,000 recruits passing through the fort each month. During the years of World War II, more than 300,000 military personnel were processed at Fort McDowell before departure to battlefields in the Pacific. The population of the fort was so large at times that a barracks was constructed to house 1,000 men with a mess hall that could seat 1,400. That building and several others that formed Fort McDowell still stand in a state of arrested decay in an area designated the "east garrison."

As the population of the island expanded in the late 1800s, the need for a civilian hospital was recognized as increasing numbers of immigrants arrived in the Bay Area carrying infectious diseases. In 1891, a quarantine station was established in Ayala Cove that eventually comprised forty buildings including a detention barracks, disinfection plant, laboratories, and rooms for staff. The Navy vessel USS *Omaha* was anchored in the cove to generate steam used to fumigate clothing and bedding. Ships arriving from China and other far eastern locations were required to anchor in the cove and present all passengers and crew for a fourteen-day quarantine process. Ships were fumigated with steam, cyanide, and burning sulfur to kill the bacteria responsible for disease and the rats that carried them. During the bubonic plague that spread through San Francisco's Chinatown in 1900–1904, infected residents were transported to Angel Island, where 119 died.

By 1946, the quarantine station was considered obsolete, as better decontamination services could be provided in San Francisco and Oakland. Today, only four buildings remain standing. The main hospital building is currently the island's visitor center and museum.

From 1914 to 1940, the immigration station on Angel Island served as the major Pacific Coast entry point for nearly 500,000 people arriving from all over the world. The facility included a large dormitory, defining halls, a hospital, a collection of cottages for staff, and interrogation rooms. Between 1915 and 1924, one third of the new arrivals were non-Asians. Increasing numbers of immigrants included Mexicans escaping civil war in their country, Russians fleeing the Bolshevik Revolution, and others from around the Pacific Rim. With the U.S. declaration of war in 1917, more than 800 alien enemies were incarcerated on the island, including German citizens residing in America and sympathizers accused of radical political activities. In addition to rigorous health inspections, lengthy and intense interrogations were performed during long periods of isolation to identify "unfit" or "dangerous" persons. Other populations at the immigration station were also subjected to health inspection and interviewed, often ending in denial of entry due to characteristics deemed "undesirable." In 1918, 148 crewmen from German merchant vessels arrived in San Francisco Bay. U.S. authorities did not label these men as prisoners of war, but they were held in isolation until transfer to North Carolina.

The station now stands as a museum dedicated to preserving the stories of Asian immigrants who endured hostile discrimination by administrators of the Chinese Exclusion Act of 1882, which remained in effect until 1943. The Immigration Station has become known as a place filled with the negative energy due to misery, fear, sorrow, and suicide endured by thousands of Asian immigrants who later contributed greatly to the culture of the Bay Area and other parts of the nation. Their experience is memorialized by the re-creation of their dormitories complete with clothing and artifacts that give visitors the impression that the center is still in operation.

Angel Island is easily accessible by ferryboat from Tiburon. The best way to explore the island's numerous ruins and historical points of interest is by bicycle. A small bookstore at Hospital Cover offers maps, guidebooks, and brief histories of island events. For visitor information, contact AngelIslandStatePark.com. Contact the Tiburon Ferry at 415-435-7679. From March through November tram, tours are available (415-435-3392).

FIRST MURDER ON ANGEL ISLAND

Hospital Cove

The first murder on Angel Island occurred at Hospital Cove (now called Ayala Cove) in 1854 when two men argued over ownership of a boat. A local fisherman, Eddie Fiefirst, attempted to dismantle a boat that he jointly owned with Captain Edward Payne. A search for Eddie's personal history has not turned up any explanation for his action or information about his partnership with the captain. It is likely that Eddie lived in a shack on the island and leased the boat from Payne, who operated a ferry between Tiburon and Ayala Cove.

After the initial clash, which included a fistfight that only served to enrage both men, they dashed away from the beach to retrieve their guns. When still quite a distance from each other, they started firing. As they continued walking toward each other, they reloaded and fired another shot. Since they were using single-shot revolvers, the reloading process would take at least forty-five seconds and the accuracy of the weapons would be poor, sparing each man from taking a bullet. Eventually, the distance between the men closed, and Captain Payne was mortally wounded. It is likely that the captain was carried to the nearby hospital, where he died.

Paranormal investigators claim that the captain's ghost still roams Hospital Cove near the waterline and shows up when small boats are beached. While walking the beach, sensitives have experienced the isolated rush of cold air that could not be attributed to prevailing breezes. Also, the muted sound of heavy boots walking on wet sand has been heard by people meditating on the beach directly in line with the lone palm tree.

DUELING FRIENDS

Quarry Point

In 1858, two friends, U.S. Commissioner George Pen Johnston (1825–1884) and State Senator William I. Ferguson (1825–1858), dueled at Quarry Point in front of one thousand spectators. The reason for the duel is unclear, despite several statements by contemporary writers including San Francisco editor Oscar T Shuck; W.H. Herndon, law partner of Abraham Lincoln; and California State Assemblyman Colonel E.D. Baker, as well as comments included in a eulogy by Reverend J.A. Benton. One account suggests that a political disagreement over the issue of slavery led to intense animosity and anger between the men that severely stressed their friendship. Another states that Johnston was enraged when Ferguson insulted a lady with whom he was "well acquainted." The woman in question was likely Sabin Francis Lewis

(1821–1876), since accounts of her death indicate that she was buried with George Pen Johnston at the Masonic Cemetery in San Francisco.

Prior to this tragic event, the young men had served together as Democrats in the California State Assembly. In 1856, Johnston was regarded as party leader and forceful debater with brilliant prospects for a long political career. At the end of the legislative session, he was promoted to commissioner of the U.S. Circuit Court. In August 1858, Ferguson arrived in San Francisco and encountered Johnston in a waterfront establishment that may have been a brothel. Apparently, their conversation became contentious and then argumentative, leading to unremitting anger. Both men, being educated and above brawling, challenged each other to a duel. A site on Angel Island, Quarry Point, was chosen possibly because dueling was illegal in California at the time and the men may have expected that the remote location would prevent interference by city police.

On August 21, the men stood facing each other with pistols in hand in front of a large gathering of friends, political supporters, and morbidly curious onlookers. Being the aggrieved party, Johnston chose single-shot pistols perhaps with the knowledge that Ferguson had never fired a gun. The first exchange of shots missed. With the second, Ferguson was wounded in the hip while a bullet grazed Johnston's abdomen. The third exchange missed, but the fourth landed a bullet in Ferguson's right thigh, probably severing the femoral artery. Stunned by the sight of his friend falling to the ground, Johnston rushed to his side, begging forgiveness.

Ferguson's doctors insisted that amputation of his right leg was essential for his survival, but he refused the operation. By September 14, however, he finally realized that he would die unless he consented to the surgery. With anesthesia by chloroform, Drs. Angle, Sawyer, Rowell, Coit, and Gray performed the amputation, but Ferguson's weakened condition, probably from sepsis, led to his death before the operation could be completed.

During the twenty-two days between the duel and Ferguson's death, George Johnston stayed with his friend, encouraging him to survive while begging forgiveness. It was reported that during this time Ferguson refused to speak to George. Despite the illegality of the duel, Johnston was acquitted of wrongful death, creating a deep sorrow in the man and leaving him embittered until his death in 1884. His deep regret of the duel was mentioned in newspaper articles of the time and in a eulogy presented at Johnston's funeral.

Now, a brooding ghost, believed to be William Ferguson, wanders the plateau above Quarry Point, harboring resentment and anger toward his former friend. Intense imprints remain at the site, likely created by horrified witnesses and the victim. Some paranormal experts believe that the ghost of George Johnston haunts the site, seeking an encounter with his former friend and forgiveness for taking his life that was denied him while alive.

HMS *RACCOON*

Launched in 1808, the HMS *Raccoon* still drifts into Hospital Cove at Angel Island, amazing witnesses who have never seen a twenty-gun British sloop of war. The *Raccoon* (Brits spelled the name with two Cs) arrived in San Francisco Bay on March 13, 1814, after a harrowing journey from the mouth of the Columbia River, where a large portion of its keel had been ripped away by powerful currents that swept the vessel over a rocky sandbar. Leaking badly and sailing poorly, its desperate crew headed south, hoping to arrive at the Spanish port of San Francisco, where repairs could be made. The harrowing journey most certainly aroused intense energy from the crew and its captain, William Black, and this may have created the phantom image of the ship still seen today.

Upon arrival in the bay, Captain Black intended to beach the vessel at the Spanish presidio, but wind and currents prevented a landing. Instead, the *Raccoon* drifted to a straight between Angel Island and Tiburon, where the winded shifted and current slacked enough to allow the vessel to be beached. Apparently, the remarkable feat of sailing a sinking ship five hundred miles and successfully bringing it to a safe landing at Angel Island inspired locals to name the narrow straight after the beleaguered vessel.

Records show that the *Raccoon* departed San Francisco on March 19, 1814, and joined a British flotilla off the coast of Chile before returning to Britain. There, in 1819, it was converted to a convict hospital ship until 1838, when it was sold and became lost to history. The *Raccoon* still drifts into Hospital Cove when heavily overcast skies dim the late afternoon light. Paranormal experts believe that the intense energy generated by a crew, facing certain of death yet delivered to a heavenly sanctuary on Angel Island, has preserved the transparent image of the battered vessel.

GHOST OF THE OLD LADY

Camp Reynolds

With the outbreak of the Civil War, fears of a Confederate attack on the Pacific Coast prompted the U.S. Army to construct extensive defensive facilities on Angel Island. A site on the southwest side of the island, facing the Golden Gate, was selected for the installation of heavy artillery and a camp that could house up to five hundred soldiers and families of officers. By 1863, Camp Reynolds was composed of fifty buildings that included officers' cottages, barracks, mess halls, a warehouse, armories, a wharf, and a large parade ground. In addition to artillery in the camp, gun batteries were placed at Points Stuart, Knox, and Blunt. Throughout the remainder of the Civil War, no Confederate vessels attempted to enter the bay.

After the Civil War, the camp was used as a recruiting and training center to stage troops for service in wars against Indian tribes including the Apaches, Modocs, and Sioux. Early in the twentieth centuries, gun emplacements were updated with the addition of three batteries equipped with modern weapons. In 1910, the camp was enlarged, making it the world's largest and most advanced military induction center. During the World War I years, personnel from the camp supported prisoner of war operations at the Immigration Station. This service was expanded during World War II as Japanese, German, and Italian prisoners were incarcerated on the island. By July 1946, however, military activity on the island had become minimal, prompting the Army to close its facilities and declare the entire island "surplus property."

Today, only eleven buildings remain at the camp, including the brick warehouse at the edge of the bay and officers' cottages and the commander's residence facing the parade ground. During my first visit to Camp Reynolds, I spotted a ghost on the porch of a house, seventh in a row facing the parade ground. The apparition was that of an old woman dressed in a black gown, seated in a rocking chair. This full-body apparition appeared quite lifelike but made no sign that she was aware of my presence. As I moved closer to the porch, I noticed the rocking chair moving slowly and the ghostly woman focusing her gaze at the bay at the end of the parade ground. Standing at about six feet from the porch, I noticed that there were no stairs. As I moved closer, the ghost's head moved as if she were about to look at me, and then she disappeared.

I waited several minutes for this ghost to reappear, but that did not happen during this visit. One year later, I returned to Camp Reynolds and stood facing the porch, waiting for a ghostly manifestation. An apparition did not appear, but as I walked the porch, I encountered an icy cold column of air in the spot where the ghostly woman previously appeared. I suspect that this ghostly woman was awaiting the return of her husband from service in the Indian Wars or the Spanish-American War.

The most tragic event to take place at Camp Reynolds was the murder of Emma Spohrs on May 23, 1872. At the age of fifteen years, Emma was the belle of the island. On the evening of her death, Emma attended a dinner and dance staged to honor Company H, scheduled to depart the island within a few days. She was escorted by her father but followed about by an unwelcome admirer, Sergeant Fritz Kimmel. According to witness accounts, Emma ignored Kimmel's advances all evening. At about midnight, he walked to her left side, placed a gun at her temple and pulled the trigger. Within moments, he turned the gun on himself and fired. Emma was buried at the Camp Reynolds cemetery in grave no. 45. For some inexplicable reason, Kimmel was buried in grave no. 46.

Official records state that all of the graves—including those of Emma and Kimmel—were removed to the mainland in 1947 to the Golden Gate National Cemetery in San Bruno. Bizarre light anomalies and other creepy sensations suggest that some of the bodies were not removed.

The site of the former cemetery is near Battery Wallace (GPS coordinates 37.85775, -122.44019), about 100 feet from the ruins of the gun emplacements and 450 feet from the camp's chapel. The cemetery was once surrounded by a picket fence that enclosed 143 graves. A few graves were marked with stone monuments, but most were made of wood. Not all of the cemetery's residents died on the island. About 35 graves contained the remains of prisoners who died on Alcatraz. The rocky nature of that island made establishment of a cemetery impossible.

Fourteen children who died before their third birthday were buried in the cemetery. They were joined by murder victim Emma Spohrs, four suicides, two drownings, one who died by an accidental wound to the neck, and six bodies that were found on the beach, deposited by the tide.

Paranormal investigators familiar with the history of cemetery relocations in the San Francisco region will question whether all of the bodies buried on Angel Island were actually removed by contracted workers. In the earlier twentieth century, thirty-five cemeteries were removed from the city of San Francisco. City leaders cited concerns over transmission of bubonic plague by diseased corpses, but it is more likely that the real estate was more valuable as sites for commercial buildings and homes. Contractors hired for the project clearly cut corners, leaving many bodies buried while removing only the headstones. There have been many instances where construction crews uncovered graves that were supposed to have been moved to cemeteries in Oakland and Coloma. So it would not be surprising to uncover paranormal evidence of bodies at the Angel Island cemetery.

GHOSTS OF THE SICK SOLDIERS

Camp Reynolds Hospital

The Camp Reynolds hospital stands on a bluff overlooking the camp. Constructed of brick during the Civil War, its three stories rise above a basement, with a single-story extension that once provided staff quarters. This building is considered structurally unsafe. Its windows and doors are boarded. The derelict appearance of the place is foreboding, giving even the most adventurous explorer the impression that breaking into the place is not wise. During one of my visits to the island, I climbed onto the balcony attached to the staff quarters. Stepping carefully over decayed floorboards, I tapped, in a sequence of three, on the boards covering the windows and doors. Certain that no one could be inside the structure, I was surprised when my taps were answered by an identical three taps. Calling out to the entity within the building, I did not receive a vocal reply.

Years later, I explored the old hospital with the *Ghost Adventures* crew. We arrived on site about midnight, a cold wind whipping across the ruddy ground in front of the place. As host Zak Bagans and I talked about the history of the place, I wondered if an investigation limited to the exterior would satisfy their viewers. I was surprised when Zak informed me that we had permission to enter the building. As sheets of plywood were pulled away from the main door, I climbed onto the balcony. As I approached the narrow passage into the building, a gust of stale, musty air emerged. The National Park Service guard standing nearby said that no one had been inside the place for thirty years.

TV crew members Aaron Goodwin and Billy Tolley and I entered the hallway and found piles of bird and bat droppings, paint peeling from the

Camp Reynolds hospital was investigated by the author with the *Ghost Adventures* TV crew.

walls and ceilings, and pungent breezes flowing out of the exam rooms and offices. Upstairs, we found a large room that was used to sequester patients with infectious diseases such as smallpox and yellow fever. As I slipped into a meditative state with the intension of empathic perception of the suffering of patients, a swarm of bats emerged from the rafters of the ceiling. The film crew left the room quickly, while I lagged behind. As the bats settled into the rafters, I moved slowly toward the doorway and heard a raspy voice say, "Don't go."

As the crew moved about the main floor, I descended a littered stair into the basement, where I discovered the morgue and operating room. Standing in the morgue, I realized that the bodies of fifteen-year-old Emma Spohr and her murderer, Fritz Kimmel, were likely brought there on May 23, 1872. I could not perceive an imprint that might be linked to them, but the room had a sickening odor of rotting flesh. With the film crew one floor above me, no audio or video was captured in the morgue or the adjacent operating room.

While exploring the operating room, I perceived the familiar odor of rotting flesh and urine. Since this room was free of bats and animal droppings, I wondered if these odors were imprints created by operations performed with crude anesthesia that failed to save lives.

We left the hospital building at about 2:00 a.m. The park service guard promptly nailed the door coverings back in place. I did not get the impression that the building was structurally unsafe, but most of the rooms contained substances that are likely hazardous and there is no electric lighting. Ghost hunters will have to limit their investigation of this haunted hospital to the exterior.

COMMUNITY OF MISERY

Immigration Station

Most of the active ghosts and fascinating paranormal phenomena on Angel Island can be found at the Immigration Station, known as the North Garrison. Located one mile east of Ayala Cove and often referred to as the "Ellis Island of the West," the center was opened in 1910 primarily to control the flow of Chinese and other Asian immigrants into the United States. Since the Chinese Exclusion Act of 1882, Chinese were generally unwelcome, and entry into the country was allowed only if immigrants could produce proof that they were related to U.S. citizens.

When ships arrived in San Francisco and Oakland, passengers from European countries were quickly processed at the gate and allowed to travel freely. Immigration officers detained Japanese, Chinese, and other Asian immigrants together with Mexicans, Russians, and South Americans and transported them to Angel Island's immigration station. Most of the immigrants underwent a long and stressful period of examination that would include undressing for a physical examine to rule out disease, hours of interrogation by teams of interpreters supervised by armed soldiers, extensive review of identity certificates, and contact of relatives currently living in the United States to confirm marriage or employment. In many cases, this process would take several days, while some immigrants were detained at the station for nearly two years. Diaries of immigrants reveal the extent of humiliation of repeated physical exams and the extreme stress inflicted by relentless interrogators. Those who arrived with forged papers, concocted stories of relatives living in the United States, or signs of disease were returned to their country of origin.

Between 1910 and 1940, nearly 500,000 immigrants, including175,000 Chinese, were examined at the center. Housed in barracks, many homesick,

Angel Island's immigrant detention center is haunted by the suicide bride.

frustrated, angry immigrants scratched poems and other graffiti on the walls. During restoration of the facility, great care was taken to preserve some of these inscriptions. One anonymous writer left this poem:

The young children do not yet know worry
Arriving at [San Francisco], *they were imprisoned in the wooden building*
Not understanding the sad and miserable situation before their eyes
They still want to play all day like calves

Many of the poems reflect the anguish of separation from family and shame from denigration to the status of cattle Contemporary interpreters of the Chinese experience report that many of those incarcerated at the center were so fearful of being turned away and sent back to the poverty they experienced in China that they committed suicide. Decades after entry to the United States, some of Angel Island's immigrants documented their experiences in books, audio histories, and video documentaries. Many of those who bravely recalled the most harrowing days of their lives agreed that the greatest fears they faced on a daily basis were "the ghosts and the starving."

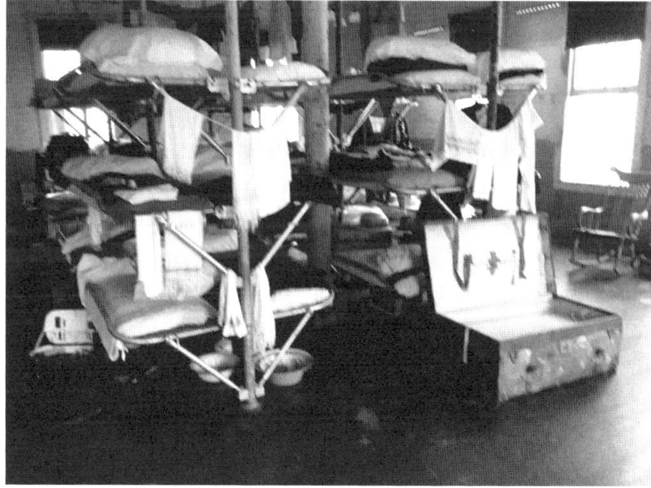

Top: Chinese wall carvings of poetry convey memories of misery.

Bottom: Detention center barracks restored to represent the immigrant experience in 1930.

The intense, repetitive emotions experienced by detainees have left several imprints in the barracks. Some of these were created during the smallpox epidemic and other periods when illnesses swept through the facility. Decades of neglect and years of restoration have not erased hundreds of paranormal imprints of muted voices speaking in Asian languages, humming, singing, sobbing, screaming, and moaning. Ghost hunters who perform EVP tests at the barracks and elsewhere on the Immigration Station's grounds should remember that most detainees did not speak English. Some sensitives pick up the peculiar odors of people living in close quarters and Chinese food. The intense impression of sadness is a common experience that sometimes includes audio perceptions of creaking floorboards, doors opening and closing, and the fragrance of Chinese herbs.

Apparitions of Chinese and other Asian immigrants dressed in their traditional clothing have been spotted walking the halls of the barracks. Witnesses report that these apparitions are nearly lifelike but appear for only a few seconds. They are often preceded by the sound of cloth slippers sliding on the wood floor.

In the Immigration Station hospital, the ghosts of patients have been spotted walking the floors with canes and crutches. While standing in the doorway of the operating room, I witnessed the ghost of a nurse walk past me.

The huge detention center, standing at the head of the wharf, burned in 1940. The cause of the fire was never clearly identified, but some historians speculate that the blaze was intentionally set by a disgruntled immigrant who had been denied entry into the country. Others suggest faulty wiring or poor maintenance was the cause. Today, the former site of the building has been landscaped as a park, with tablets commemorating the historical events of immigrant arrivals. The barracks remains as a fascinating museum restored to the 1920s, depicting the environment in which thousands of immigrants awaited entry to the United States. Ruins of the staff cottages and other structures are worthy targets for ghost hunters.

GHOST OF THE CHINESE BRIDE

Immigration Station

A haunting sustained by strong, durable energy occurs in the bathroom of the women's dormitory. Known as the ghost of the Chinese bride, this spirit manifestation has been occurring for more than a century. It was first reported by Chinese women living in the dormitory in about 1918 whose written statements and oral histories clearly indicate that the two worst things about the immigration station were "the ghosts and the starving."

The ghost is that of a young Chinese woman who emigrated from China with the intention of meeting a man in San Francisco with whom marriage had been arranged. Typical of the time, immigration officials doubted the authenticity of her letters and documents since many people trying to enter the country at the time used forged documents and false identities. Consequently, the young woman was interrogated several times by officials, who doubted her story and were unable to confirm the marriage arrangement with people in the Chinese community in the city. It has been reported that the interrogation was severe, lasting hours with harsh accusations. When the young woman was informed that her entry into the United States was denied, she returned to the dormitory, put on her wedding dress, and walked into the bathroom. Using a bed sheet, she created a noose and hanged herself.

When her lifeless body was discovered, the fear and anxiety suffered by the women in the dormitory became overwhelming. They demanded that lights be kept on throughout the night. Several months passed before the residents of the dormitory were released into the United States or returned to China. By then, the story of the suicide bride had become legend, and the story was passed down through new immigrants until the stations closed in 1946.

Years later, oral histories preserved the event and the reactions of women who resided in the dormitory at the time. Many women reported the sensation of an unseen presence in the bathroom where lights would flicker off and on. Some women were afraid to enter the bathroom alone because of an intense foreboding of something fearful and sad that aggravated their own anxiety. One of the dormitory's occupants reported that she was awakened one night by an unseen entity leaning over her as she lay in bed. The entity's hands pressed firmly on her chest, giving the frightened woman the impression that something was attacking her. Unable to breath, she tried to scream, but she could not make a sound. Panicked, she whispered a prayer that ended the attack.

More recently, sensitive people who enter the bathroom become acutely aware of an intense sadness that causes some empaths to immediately leave the room. Many report a change in the atmosphere and the impression that there is something very negative about the place. The apparition of the young bride has not been spotted, nor have paranormal investigators captured EVPs. Since visitors, including ghost hunters, are not allowed to view the bathroom, it is uncertain if the ghost is still active at the site.

When we filmed a *Ghost Adventures* episode on the island, I anticipated that the crew would investigate this ghost story and capture some compelling evidence. Unfortunately, the shooting schedule did not allow time to experience the ghost of the Chinese bride.

GHOSTS AND SATANIC RITUALS

Fort McDowell

Fort McDowell stands today as a collection of derelict buildings, some in a state of arrested decay and others seemingly on the verge of collapse. Many are not accessible to the public due to structural concerns or risk of hazardous substances. Some buildings give the impression that they were damaged by a military battle, while others have been renovated and used as housing for people who work on the island.

This fort had its origins late in the nineteenth century as an extension of Camp Reynolds. Designated the "East Garrison," the facility was used as a detention facility. Inmates worked at a nearby quarry that supplied stones for expansion of the military fort. In 1899, the population of the fort grew exponentially as troops were trained for the Spanish-American War in the Pacific. Two years later, the fort was primarily a quarantine center for troops returning to America with yellow fever and other infectious diseases. The Thirty-First Volunteer Infantry Division returned with smallpox. Other military units brought venereal diseases and PTSD.

By April 1900, the camp had grown so large that it was designated as a singular military establishment and renamed Fort McDowell, an homage to General Irvin MacDowell (1818–1885), leader of the Union army at the Battle of Bull Run. Apparently, the general had close ties to the Bay Area,

Fort McDowell on Angel Island.

having served as commanding officer of the Department of the Pacific while stationed at the Presidio of San Francisco.

In the first five years of the twentieth century, nearly twelve thousand soldiers were processed for entry to or discharge from military service at Fort McDowell. Another eighty-seven thousand passed through the camp en route to destinations throughout the western Pacific and Central America.

In 1909, military prisoners housed on Alcatraz were transported to Angel Island to bolster a workforce that built a 600-man barrack, mess halls seating 1,400 soldiers, officers' quarters, a guardhouse, a hospital and other buildings. These facilities were heavily used during World War II as more than 300,000 soldiers passed through the fort before shipping out to the war in the Pacific.

Today, many buildings stand as a haven for ghosts of those who died in the hospital from wounds sustained in battle, infectious disease, accidents, and suicide. The hospital is a prime target for local ghost hunters because of the high frequency of paranormal activity that includes ethereal images of patients walking around in bloodied hospital gowns, soldiers in blue uniforms, and doctors wearing surgical outfits. Other experiences include unexplained lights and that creepy feeling that an unseen being is standing close by. Vocalizations captured on audio recorders include slamming doors, heavy footsteps, sound bursts of screams, moans, and sobbing. Each floor of the hospital included exterior hallways, affording ghost hunters opportunities to see the apparitions of the hospital without entering a derelict building that contain hazards like animal droppings. Hundreds of visitors to this creepy old building report bizarre impressions of sickening odors, cells of cold air, and a sense of danger.

Early in my career as a paranormal investigator, I gained access to the Administration Center. Entering the building alone, I was instantly aware of several people walking through the lobby and adjacent hallways. Most of these apparitions were dressed in military uniforms and appeared unaware of my presence. These ghostly images came into view, walked twenty or thirty feet, and then faced away. I did not perceived auditory phenomena, but the multiple apparitions walking in several directions while crossing the lobby gave me the impression that they were ghosts that remained on duty, completely unaware they had died. Today, the Administration Center is not accessible, but ghost hunters may get a good view of the interior through several open windows.

While filming *Ghost Adventures* at Fort McDowell, the crew entered one of the officer's apartments located on a ridge overlooking the entire

The Fort McDowell hospital is haunted by ghosts of patients and nurses.

military facility. Some of the apartments in the row are used as housing for Angel Island staff, including National Park Service rangers. Inside one of the apartments, several satanic symbols were found painted on the walls. Although the meaning of the symbols and the intention of the artist who created them are not known, their appearance gave the entire crew an intensely discomforting feeling. In one of the apartments, a moving toy was captured on video. While the crew investigated the second floor of the apartment, a static camera captured a small doll fly off the shelf. Later, during debriefing, many members of the production crew reported that they had perceived a warning that they were not welcome in the rooms.

CHAPTER 5
MARE ISLAND

For nearly one thousand years before the first Europeans enter San Francisco Bay in 1769, Native American tribes in the region used Mare Island as a camp for fishing and hunting geese and ducks. Remnants of their activity on the island have been found in shell mounds that reveal the kinds of fish that were caught and shells harvested, along with tools, hunting gear, weapons, cooking devices, and even human remains. With the arrival of Spanish explorers in 1769, Native Americans visited the island less frequently to avoid contact with people who sailed in large ships and carried weapons of unimaginable power. Despite Spanish exploration of the bay and eventual annexation, no forts or settlements were established on Mare Island. There is some speculation that the Spanish constructed a crude jail on the island at a site near the Marine Barracks, but no archaeological evidence has been found of a structure dating from the Spanish period.

After the transfer of California from Spain to Mexico in 1820, squatters moved onto the island, including Victorio Castro, who grazed sheep; goat shepherd William Bryant; and a Major Cooper, who, in 1830, brought dairy cows to the island. In 1832, General Mariano Vallejo received a land grant from the Mexican government of 175,000 acres, which included Mare Island and portions of today's Sonoma County. With such vast holdings, the general did not develop the island, but squatters were required to pay rent. In 1832, a barge attempting the cross Carquinez Strait with a cargo of horses foundered in rough water and capsized. When word of the event reached General Vallejo, he was devastated when he learned that his prize mare was among the horses thrown into the bay waters. Days later, fishermen spotted a mare running along the shores of the island. When the animal was recognized as the general's mare, the island became known as Mare Island.

Mare Island remained a place of little consequence until 1852, when Secretary of the Navy William Graham ordered Commodore David Sloat to establish a naval shipyard on the West Coast. By 1853, the Navy had purchased 956 acres of waterfront land and constructed a floating dry dock. By September 1854, the Navy had begun shipbuilding and repair under the command of Commander David Farragut (1808–1870). Under his command, Mare Island grew into a major naval facility that included several building that still stand today, including a smithery, Building 46 (1856); a warehouse, Building 71 (1858); a foundry, Building 85 (1858); a boiler shop, designated Building 89/91 (1858); and an ordnance magazine, Building A1 (1857). After Farragut's departure in 1862 to command a naval squadron, the shipyard continue to grow with the addition of more than 150 buildings and four dry docks that could accommodate ships up to seven hundred feet in length. The first ship build at Mare Island, a paddle-wheel gunboat named the *Saginaw*, was launched in 1859 and preceded several hundred ships to be built at the shipyard, including several nuclear-powered submarines.

With the onset of the Spanish-American War (1898) and World War I, the shipyard underwent intense modernization with expansion of fabrication facilities and a workforce that included hundreds of civilians. By 1941, the navy base comprised 996 building, including a large hospital, schools for firefighters, and other special services performed by naval personnel. During the World War II years, as many as fifty thousand civilians and thirty-nine thousand naval personnel worked in the shipyards, constructing 391 ships and repaired 1,227 battle-damaged ships that returned to duty in the Pacific.

During the Cold War years (1947–91), Mare Island shipyard workers constructed seventeen nuclear-powered submarines, including the first vessel of its kind built on the West Coast, the USS *Sargo*, in 1954. The yard also constructed the USS *Vallejo* in 1966, honoring the former owner of Mare Island.

Despite Mare Island shipyard's capacities and the technical expertise of its vast workforce, including mechanical and nuclear engineers, the base was closed in 1993, and naval operations ended in 1996. Many of the buildings, dry docks, and other facilities have since been leased by private companies to carry on ship repair operations. One of the largest buildings on Mare

Island was converted to a movie sound stage where Eddie Murphy's *Metro* (1997) was filmed, followed by the sci-fi blockbuster *Sphere* (1998) and Robin Williams's *What Dreams May Come* (1998).

Today, several historic buildings, dry docks, and other structures offer ghost hunters a vast array of venues for paranormal experiences. In 1900, a row of twelve mansions was constructed to serves as quarters for high-ranking officers. Standing four stories tall and offering more than six thousand square feet of living space, the mansions were constructed with ornate oak woodwork, massive staircases, and spacious rooms designed to impress foreign dignitaries and members of Congress visiting the shipyards. Two of the mansions—Quarters N and Quarters O—are accessible to the public as a coffee shop and wine tasting venue, respectively. Quarters A, used by the highest-ranking admiral on the island, is nearly eight thousand square feet and is open for tours and special events.

Other venues for ghost hunting include the old prison, warehouse Building 77, the Mare Island Historical Park museum, the stables, dry dock no. 1, the Naval Cemetery, bomb shelters on Nereus Avenue, and ammunition depots that include Building A-199, used to storage high explosives used in World War II.

The history of Mare Island venues includes numerous accidents, disasters, untimely deaths, and other events that have generated reports of negative energy and intense paranormal activity throughout the shipyard. Imprints of misery, pain, and anger experienced by prisoners fill the old prison to the extent that one expert ghost hunter reported the place to be crowded with so much negative energy that a visit of more than five minutes could not be tolerated.

Paranormal activity in the shipyard's cemetery is attributed to victims of the 1892 munitions explosion that killed fifteen crewmen from the USS *Boston*. The warship sailed into Mare Island for repairs, which required all munitions to be offloaded. While the crew prepared the gunpowder for storage in a warehouse, an explosion occurred that was so great that the bodies of two crewmen were found on a beach two hundred yards from the site of the disaster. Navy investigators attributed the explosion to a dropped shell that caused a spark, igniting gunpowder that littered the floor like fine dust. A local ghost hunting team, Chill Seekers, captured EVP in the cemetery at the USS *Boston* monument that revealed the names of the two crewmen who may have been responsible for the disaster: Joos and Ostrander. These names, spoken by spirits and captured on a recording device, may be found among the list of crewmen on the USS *Boston* monument in the cemetery.

Another explosion occurred on July 9, 1917, at the gunpowder magazine at the Naval Munition Depot that killed six people and destroyed thirteen buildings. Historians have uncovered information that raises suspicion of sabotage carried out by a group of German double agents as World War I raged in Europe. One man, Ordnanceman Neil Damstedt, was killed inside the building as he swept the floor. Parts of his body were found several yards south of the munitions magazine, while his head landed far to the north. The explosion also killed James and Malvina Mackenzie and their three children, Allan, Dorothy, and Mildred, as the blasted ripped through their house. This family are interred at the Mare Island cemetery.

More recently, the Spanish flu epidemic of 1918–20 filled the shipyard's hospital with desperately ill people. The exact death toll is not known, but it likely reached twenty military personnel and civilians admitted to the hospital out of thousands treated for the disease. Hospital records of other illness and injuries that led to deaths of shipyards workers in not accessible. Given the dangerous work in the dry docks, foundries, fabrication buildings, cranes, and shops, it seems likely that hundreds of people—military personnel and civilians—died on Mare Island, leaving a paranormal legacy that is easily accessed by dedicated ghost hunters

THE SAD GHOST: LIEUTENANT SAM WILSON

Building 77
Nereus at Connolly Street

Burial errors sit high on the list of events that may trap a ghost on the physical plane or entice a ghost to remain at a specific site. Placement of the deceased's body in the wrong grave is the most common blunder, but leaving a corpse grated in a warehouse for seven years is far more injurious to the spirit and likely to create a lot of anger. This is the unconscionable treatment suffered by Lieutenant Sam Wilson (1844–1879), who died while serving in the Navy in China. At the age of thirty-five, Sam died on August 1, 1879, on board his ship anchored in Yokohama Harbor. The official cause of death was listed as a neurological condition that triggered an epileptic fit. The Navy buried Sam with full military honors in Japan and sent the requisite War Department telegram to his wife, Rosalyn, who resided on the

Mare Island Building 77 was constructed in 1870.

East Coast. A few years later, Sam's casket was exhumed, grated, and sent to Mare Island for reburial at the shipyard's cemetery. There is conflicting information about why this happen. One story suggested that Sam's wife made the request and purchased a headstone to be placed at his Mare Island grave site. Amateur historian Lauren Martins uncovered contemporary newspaper articles that indicate a campaign, of sorts, possibly launched by friends and shipmates, to bring Sam home. Despite widespread support for Sam's posthumous repatriation, it seems that no one noticed the arrival of his casket. Crated and resembling hundreds of others offloaded from the ship, Sam's remains were placed in Building 77, where they remained for seven years. When the casket was finally discovered, Sam was buried at the Naval Cemetery on August 8, 1887. It is unknown if his headstone was purchased by his wife, who had remarried, or the Navy.

It is likely that Sam Wilson was unaware of his reburial in the cemetery and that his ghost, still trapped in Building 77, was angry at the treatment his corpse had received. For many years after discovery of his casket, workers in Building 77 experienced many strange events. Fire alarms would sound for no apparent reason, lights flickered, and bizarre groans and shouts were heard that resembled a man in agony. Workers in the building suffered several accidents, and tools would often go missing only to be found in inexplicable places. Paranormal activity inside the building became so disturbing that the shipyard commandant ordered the lights to be kept on 24/7. Sam's ghostly activity persisted until the late 1980s and was nearly forgotten as the shipyard's workforce diminished in the 1990s.

The location inside Building 77 where Lieutenant Sam Wilson's body was stored in a crate for seven years.

Decades after shipyard closure, I was granted access to Building 77 to determine if Sam Wilson's ghost still resided there. Prior to my visit, I learned that the exact location where Sam's crated coffin sat in the building was unknown. Using dowsing rods, EMF detectors, and psychic sensitivity, I discovered that the spot was midway along the south wall, near the double doors. At this location, dowsing rods were highly active, and I detected a dense cell of cold air that registered ten to twelve degrees cooler than adjacent air. EVP captured on audio recorders were not sufficiently clear to identify specific words, but a male voice was heard.

Sam Wilson has become somewhat of a folk hero among many who work to preserved Mare Island history. Much sympathy has been directed at the Sam, but the history of his brief life suggests that he was an unconventional man. Following graduation from the Naval Academy in 1864, Sam was moved from one duty station to another with very brief periods on several ships. In 1873, he was sued for seducing another man's wife and escaped further legal action by paying $150. While stationed at Mare Island on the USS *Independence* in 1875, Sam was court-martialed for being absent without leave (AWOL), furloughed for several weeks, and then restored to duty at half pay for two years. After returning to duty at Mare Island, Sam suffered the first of a number of "epileptic attacks." Navy doctors attributed these attacks to excessive alcohol consumption. In 1879, soon after his arrival in Yokohama Bay on July 20, Sam went AWOL again. Days after returning to duty aboard the USS *Ashuelot*, Sam suffered another "attack" that ended his life.

Many local historians and paranormal investigators belief that Sam Wilson's ghost haunted the cemetery. Since access to Building 77 is restricted and generally open to visitors only on special tours, people seeking the ghostly Sam Wilson can search for him in the cemetery.

A GATHERING OF SPIRITS

Mare Island Naval Cemetery
Azuar Avenue to Imhoff Road

The Naval Cemetery on Mare Island is small by military standards, but its one thousand graves tucked into 2.4 acres represent a fascinating history of the shipyard's 150 years of operation. Many of the occupants of the graves died while working at Mare Island, while others died at sea or in foreign ports and left wishes for burial at a favored duty station in the San Francisco Bay. The first burial occurred on February 12, 1856, when George Dowd (1815–1856), quartermaster of the USS *Massachusetts*, entered eternal rest one day after his death on board the ship. George's grave is not far from the final resting place of Anna Arnold Key Turner (1811–1884), daughter of Francis Scott Key, author of "The Star-Spangled Banner." Anna was one of the first teachers in the Vallejo public school system. She lies next to her husband, David (1796–1860), who arrived at Mare Island in 1854 with Commodore Farragut and worked as a supervising engineer in the construction of several buildings, some of which still stand today.

Three Medal of Honor recipients are buried at the cemetery. James Cooney (1860–1903) received his medal for bravery in combat during the Boxer Rebellion in China on July 13, 1900. His grave is located in Section D, Row 10, Plot 093. Hero of the USS *Saginaw* rescue William Halford (1841–1919) earned his place in naval history by sailing a small boat 1,500 miles to seek help for shipmates strained on the island of Kure, near Midway Island. Suffering from starvation, dehydration, and the loss of four men who began the desperate journey with him, he arrived in Kauai after thirty-one days at sea an enlisted the help of King Kamehameha to rescue the Saginaw's crew. His grave is located in Section C, Row 7, Plot 371.

Left: Mare Island Naval Cemetery, opened in 1856.

Opposite: The USS *Boston* monument stands over the common grave of fifteen sailors killed in 1892.

Alexander Parker (1832–1900), boatswain's mate on the USS *Portsmouth*, moored at Mare Island, rescued a shipmate who was drowning in the strait separating the island from Vallejo. It is unknown whom Alexander rescued, but it is likely that the man was a high-ranking officer or public official because the Medal of Honor was awarded only two weeks after the incident. Parker's grave is located at Section D, Row 13, Plot 059.

Not everyone buried in the cemetery is a hero or person of laudable historical importance. Lucy Lawson (1841–1919), also known as Louisa May "Lucy Ann" Morrison Lawson, lies in a grave in Section A, Row A1, Plot 668. In Virginia on March 15, 1875, she was convicted of hiring her cousin Anderson Shiflett to kill her husband, David. She and her conspirators were sentenced to hang, but the first execution, that of Shiflett, failed when the hangman's noose broke. A delay in the proceedings was sufficient for new testimony to be discovered that led to Lucy's stay of execution and a pardon by Governor William Cameron. Upon her release, she moved to Washington, D.C., and work as a nanny for Commodore Stacy Potts (1853–1928). When the commodore moved to Mare Island, Lucy moved with the family. In 1908, the Potts family settled into a house at 705 Georgia Street in Vallejo. Lucy died in that house in 1919, and because the commodore had retired from service at Mare Island in 1910, she was granted burial rights at the cemetery.

Two stately monuments standing in the cemetery honor the bravery and tragic demise of shipmates. The USS *Boston* monument honors fifteen sailors who died in a horrific explosion in a munitions magazine on June 13,

1892. The mass grave contains only body parts since the force of the explosion was so great that none of the victims' remains were recognizable without heads. Not far from the cemetery's entrance stands a monument to six Russian sailors who died in 1863 fighting a fire in San Francisco. Their ship, the *Bogatyr*, arrived in San Francisco Bay at the invitation of President Abraham Lincoln to counter French and British fleets that might interfere with West Coast shipping in support of the Confederacy. When a fire broke out on the near the waterfront on October 23, the ship's captain sent his entire crew to fight the fire. The six men who died occupy a single grave.

Many of the graves in this cemetery have been visited by local ghost hunters. Two graves that have received the most attention are those of the Mackenzie family (Section A, Row 01A), who died in the munitions explosion of 1917, and Lieutenant Sam Wilson (Section C, Row 03, Plot 171), whose body lay inside Building 77 for many years before burial. Amazing EVPs have been captured at these grave sites. Some adventurous ghost hunters have reports seeing inexplicable light phenomena over the graves at night despite closure of the cemetery at dusk.

A local paranormal team, Chill Seekers, reported fascinating EVPs at the Boston monument. In response to questions about the cause of the explosion, ghostly voices spoke the names of two men responsible for the tragedy: Joos and Ostrander.

The cemetery is open Monday through Friday from 8:00 a.m. to 4:30 p.m. On weekends, the gate on Azuar Avenue is closed, but visitors may walk to the cemetery. The cemetery is currently cared for by the Mare Island Shoreline Heritage Preserve (707-249-9633).

GHOST OF THE PASTOR

St. Peter's Chapel
800 Walnut Avenue
707-557-1538

U.S. Navy chaplain Reverend Adam A. McAlister (1841–1909) arrived at Mare Island in 1873 only to find makeshift facilities for religious services. After twenty-five years of staging services in various shipyard buildings that happened to be unused at the time, McAlister prevailed on U.S. Senator George C. Perkins to include a $5,000 appropriation in the 1900 Naval Appropriations Act for the construction of a chapel at Mare Island. San Francisco architect Albert Sutton created blueprints for a Gothic-style one-story, wood-frame structure capped by a gabled roof. When completed, the chapel stood as the second chapel built on U.S. Navy property and the first in the Navy's Pacific region.

A dedication ceremony of the chapel was held on October 13, 1901. In the years following its opening, twenty-seven artistic glass windows were added to the structure, including twenty-five windows from Tiffany Studios in New York. Sixteen of those windows are signed by designer Frederick Wilson. The chapel's collection of Tiffany windows is one of the largest in the United States. Interior decorations included several wall plaques commemorating Navy personnel and units lost in battle or at sea. Nearly all of the Tiffany windows were in place when Reverend McAlister's funeral was held on July 12, 1916. The reverend was buried at Mare Island cemetery (Section A, Row 02, Plot 439).

The chapel served the Mare Island community of civilian workers and Navy personnel for ninety-four years, as a venue for weddings, funerals, baptisms, and memorial services. During World War II, as many as fifteen weddings were staged each week as young sailors married their sweethearts before shipping out for the war in the Pacific. The cozy sanctuary was crowded with nearly three hundred people on Christmas Eve 1995 for the final service before closure of the base in March 1996.

Today, access to the chapel is limited to tours conducted by the Mare Island Historic Park Foundation and other special events. Many who are fortunate to spend time in the sanctuary alone report whispered voices, soft footsteps, and muted sobbing. Sensitives perceive several unseen beings moving about, sliding into the pews. Occasionally, bursts of sound are

St. Peter's Chapel on Mare Island was opened in 1901 and hosted hundreds of weddings and funnels.

perceived, including the vibrato of organ notes and a choir. In two of my visits to the chapel, I believe I encountered the ghost of Reverend McAlister. In a very brief visual experience, I saw a tall man dressed in a dark suit, without a pastor's collar. His white beard appeared as a flash of light before disappearing. Several people sitting alone in the pews have reported the sensation of an unseen person sitting next to them, occasionally with mild, noxious body odor or perfume.

GODFATHER'S MANSION

1005 Walnut Avenue
707-552-2331

The grand mansions on Walnut Avenue comprise Captain's Row, which stands today as a fascinating collection of period architecture and sanctuary for ghosts. In the nineteenth century, twelve three-story homes were constructed of brick masonry on the street to serve as quarters for the highest-ranking officers in the various commands of the shipyard. Nearly all of them were destroyed in the earthquake of 1898. Many officers believed that this was a blessing of sorts because the houses were not large and certainly not impressive. In 1900, the Navy began building grand mansions for high-ranking officers at many bases in the United States.

At Mare Island, twelve mansions were constructed on the foundations of the homes destroyed in 1898. With living space ranging from eight thousand to ten thousand square feet, these impressive four-story homes were fitted out with oak panels, ornate corbels, built-in china cabinets and bookshelves, and massive staircases. Tall columns standing on large verandas ensured that visitors would feel that they were about to enter a home occupied by a powerful commander. Each mansion included large formal and informal parlors, dining rooms that could seat twenty people, a private office, and large closets designed to accommodate the officer's collection of uniforms. Behind many of these mansions, servants' quarters were constructed together with stables for horses. Officers and their families truly lived in a luxurious fashion, provided by the U.S. Navy. Mare Island's Captain's Row is recognized as one of the most historic examples of military family housing in the United States.

Today, only three of the mansions are accessible by the public. One of them stands at 1005 Walnut Avenue and houses the Vino Godfather wine tasting room. Opened in 2015, the place is a popular gathering spot for locals who enjoy the fine wines produced by a winery founded by Frank Kennedy and his partner, Twila Nixon. On a typical weekend, wine tasters sit in the backyard, listening to local bands. Frank, known as the Godfather, was always there, surrounded by friends and admirers. Through a mutual friend, I met Frank and inquired about ghosts in the mansion. He affirmed that the place was haunted and referred me to tasting room manager Brett Mifune, who provided information about paranormal activity in the mansion.

While stacking cases of wine in the basement, a worker felt a strong hand tug on his shoulder. Thinking that a coworker had reached out to him, he turned but saw that no one had entered the basement. This experience was repeated a number of times over a period of months, becoming progressively less disturbing. While standing in the dining room, this worker also spotted a lady wearing a fancy red dress as she walked in the kitchen.

One evening, some employees were sitting in the great room when they spotted a man ascend the front stairs to the porch. Since the place was closed, one of the staff went to the door to inform the visitor. When he arrived at the door, no one could be seen on the porch. Minutes later, loud footsteps were heard on the grand staircase rising from the foyer to the second floor. Rushing to the staircase, the workers found no one there. It was later assumed that a ghost had ascended the exterior stairs, approached the front door, and then disappeared before entering the lobby and going upstairs to the second floor.

Above: Formerly an officer's mansion, this grand old house is now occupied by the Godfather winery's tasting room.

Left: The ornate interiors of the mansions on officers' row retain creepy atmospheres.

Some nights, when playing loud music while working late, employees have heard a voice shout "Get out!" Clearly, a ghost felt disturbed by the music and activity of the workers. Godfather Frank had some ghostly experiences as well. One day, he spotted a cocker spaniel running around the front parlor, crossing the foyer, and dashing behind the bar at stands in the foyer. Following the dog's route, Frank looked behind the bar but found no dog.

Brett Mifune also told me of a paranormal experience that occurred while guiding eight visitors on a tour of the mansion. While ascending a narrow stair to the attic, Brett reached for the doorknob and felt engulfed by a "strong negative feeling" that warned him not to proceed. Unnerved by the warning, Brett decided not to enter the attic. Members of the tour group volunteered that they, too, perceived a warning that reportedly said, "Stop. Do not go any further."

In October 2024, I was invited to investigate the Vino Godfather mansion, and my first objective was to enter the attic, perhaps to learn if some private or malevolent spirit occupied the space. I spent two hours in the dark attic with EMF detectors, continuous video recording, and audio recorders. I placed three colored plastic balls on the floor and invited any ghosts in the space to move them. During long periods of observation, I did not detect significant motion, although at times the balls appeared to vibrate. Audio recordings did not capture specific responses to my questions, but I did capture several vocalizations of "sh-hh," as if the ghost was insisting that I stop speaking. Dowsing rods did elicit several responses that indicate that the ghost in the attic is a man who worked in the house as a servant. Through questioning and dowsing rod responses, he claimed that he was not angry but merely wanted to be left alone so he could perform his duties.

Stairway to the haunted attic of the Godfather mansion on officers' row.

Perhaps the most bizarre event during my investigation was damage to my video camera. After forty-five minutes of operation while mounted on a tripod, the camera froze with the lens extended. After changing the batteries, the camera failed to operate. Efforts to retract the lens have been unsuccessful.

Since Frank Kennedy's death, some local ghost hunters have speculated that he might appear in the garden, taking a seat among his ardent followers. If Frank's ghost has taken up residence in the mansion, he could appear in any of its rooms.

The identity of ghosts in the mansion remains unknown. Over the ninety-five years of occupancy by several Navy families, it is likely that a tragic accident may have occurred or that an illness took the life of someone who loved the place. It is also possible that a death that occurred elsewhere liberated a ghost from its bodily confines so it could return to the grandest home it knew when alive.

QUARTERS A

Admiral's Mansion
1065 Walnut Avenue

Soon after the collapse of the Walnut Avenue officers' quarters caused by the 1898 earthquake, construction of replacement mansions began that still stand today. The centerpiece of the construction was Quarters A, intended to be the residence of the highest-ranking naval officer on Mare Island. The home was grand in design, and the porch was enclosed by four columns standing two stories high. Verandas to the left and right were graced with shorter columns. The ten-thousand-square-foot interior included large parlors, a dining room, a private office, and numerous bedrooms to accommodate the admiral's family. Quarters for house servants were placed behind the mansion.

Historical narratives suggest that the shipyard commander, Rear Admiral Kirkland (1836–1898), haunts the present-day mansion despite its construction years after his death. The popular story states that the admiral was so badly shaken by the 1898 earthquake that he ran from the house only to collapse on the front walk from a heart attack. It has been assumed that the admiral's ghost returned to the site of his home and took up residence in the new mansion constructed in 1900. Digging deeper into the history of Quarters A, I discovered that Admiral Kirkland did not die as described

Quarters 1 was the home of the admiral in command of Mare Island shipyards.

in currently available reports. Instead, the admiral developed a severe bowel condition that required surgery in San Francisco on August 9, 1898. Initially showing improvement, the admiral's condition deteriorated while he remained hospitalized until his death on August 12.

While it is possible that Admiral Kirkland returned to the Mare Island site of his former home, my research points to a more likely ghost. Rear Admiral Frank Lowry (1888–1955) commanded the Mare Island shipyard from 1947 to 1950 following an auspicious career that included directing the World War II landing at Anzio and Operation Dragoon landing of U.S. troops in southern France. He received the Navy Cross for his exceptional command of the battleship USS *Minneapolis* in the Battle of the Coral Sea (May 1942) and the Battle of Midway (June 1942). After settling into residence on Mare Island, Admiral Lowry also demonstrated exceptional skill in gardening. At his direction, more than ten thousand bricks were purchased and used to create pathways around the mansions of Walnut Avenue. Lowry also created gardens and planted trees that shaded the yards.

Admiral died in Napa on March 26, 1955, but all who knew him recognized that his most favored home was Mare Island. During his later years, he often returned to the Quarters A gardens to ensure that staff were keeping the brick pathways in good repair and properly caring for the plants.

The pale, highly transparent apparition of an adult male has been spotted standing in the shadows cast by the trees at the back of the mansion. He does not appear to move as he fades in and out of view. Ghost hunters who visit

Quarters A should also look for a ghost with Admiral Kirkland's famous red hair, for which the admiral was dubbed "Red Bill" because of the contrast with his florid complexion and fiery personality.

I investigated the interior of the mansion in January 2025. Dim lights in the massive rooms and ornate woodwork created a spooky atmosphere that was made even more chilling by the absence of anyone else in the place. In several places, I detected inexplicable cells of cold air and breezes. With all windows and doors closed and no ventilation systems running, the breezes were more like an isolated touch on the shoulder.

In the second-floor hallway, I discovered the door to the closet used by servants to hang the admiral's uniforms without entering the very private bedroom. A second door that opened to the bedroom enabled the admiral to access his uniforms. Inside the closet, I captured an EVP of a male voice that repeated the phrase "Yes, sir," to every question I asked. I concluded that this ghostly voice was that of a servant who believes he is still on duty. In the grand parlor, I captured EVPs of sound bursts of a large group of people, speaking simultaneously, as if a party were underway.

Access to Quarters A is limited to special tours or rental of the mansion for weddings and other events. The gardens and brick pathways created by Admiral Lowry may be visited with restriction.

GHOSTS OF THE WORRIED PATIENT

Mare Island Naval Hospital
Talos Avenue at Cossey Street

This stately building was once a state-of-the-art military hospital serving Mare Island naval personnel and civilian workers in addition to sick and injured brought by ships from duty stations all over the Pacific. Opened in 1901, the hospital replaced its predecessor, which was severely damaged by the 1898 earthquake. Designed to serve 250 patients, its bed capacity was increased as the working population of Mare Island grew. By the end of World War I, the hospital could accommodate up to 600 patients in crowded conditions. Capacity reached 2,300 patients during World War II as surgery units worked around the clock. By 1957, the aging facility could no longer be maintained according the naval standards. A regional

Vintage photo of the former Mare Island Naval Hospital, which opened in 1901.

medical dispensary replaced the hospital's clinics, serving a slowly declining population of shipyard workers.

In 1999, the hospital was rejuvenated by Touro University with the intention of using the grand building as a medical school. After twenty years of ongoing repairs and renovations, the building was closed. Currently, the roof is undergoing replacement, and the impressive portico is being rebuilt.

During its fifty-six years of operation, many patients died in this building. During the Spanish flu epidemic of 1918–20, the hospital cared for many people suffering from this disease. Archived California Board of Health reports from the era state that 341 people died in the Vallejo–Marie Island area. Many of them died in tents set up on the hospital grounds in order to maintain separation. During World War II, thousands of severely wounded soldiers, sailors, and marines were treated at the hospital. The number of deaths that occurred during this period remains unknown.

Access to the building is not available due to unsafe structure and ongoing repairs. Ghost hunters have captured EVPs at the main entrance, however. My recorder captured a male voice saying, "Please don't worry about me." Another voice, apparently a woman, said, "I called you here."

It is likely that hundreds of imprints from intense, repetitive emotional experiences may be discovered under the portico. It is rumored that the morgue, located in the basement, has been the site of many highly disturbing paranormal events. Efforts to verify the rumors have not been successful.

JAILED GHOSTS

Mare Island Naval Prison
Flagship Drive at Sargo Avenue

After nearly a century of dispensing justice aboard U.S. Navy ships by flogging with whips, keelhauling, allowing only bread and water, and confining offenders in a dark, damp cell overrun with rats, Congress enacted a ban on such treatments in 1850. The alternative would be a shore-side prison where the fleet's incorrigibles would be incarcerated similar to civilian prisons. Following Navy Department directives, Mare Island commanders ordered the construction of a prison, which opened in 1868. Hastily constructed in only three months, the single-story facility proved adequate for only a short time. By 1890, a second story had been added, followed by additional expansions in 1901, 1908, and 1938. Today, the old prison, dubbed "Old 84" due to its designation as shipyard building no. 84, stands derelict. Recently escaping demolition, the prison is closed to visitors, but access is occasionally permitted by the Mare Island Park Historical Foundation.

I visited the prison in September 2024 and found it dank, dark, and incredibly creepy. The prison's reputation seemed quite appropriate, although the cells had been removed and there was virtually nothing remaining in the building that would stand as a monument to its history. Soon after the place filled up with prisoners, the Mare Island facility became known as one of the worst places a sailor or marine could be sent. Guards were tough and unyielding, but the greatest threat a prisoner might face came from other prisoners. The place housed convicted deserters, mutineers, thieves, and men who conspired to kill their commanding officers. Vintage photographs revealed overcrowding and cells placed in the center of the building that prevented a view to the exterior. Among the infamous sailors incarcerated in Old 84 was Navy deserter Jack Mosby, jailed in 1912, who claimed to have held the rank of general in the Mexican rebel army. His notoriety is surpassed

Left: The infamous "Old 84" Mare Island prison.

Opposite: Mare Island prison cells have been removed, but an intense ghostly presence remains.

by George Boyog, a sailor on the USS *California*. Dubbed the "Battleship Bandit," George planned to attack the ship's purser, force him to open the safe, and then escape from the ship with thousands of dollars. Despite being armed with a pistol, knife, and bayonet, George was overpowered by guards and thrown in prison for fifteen years.

Given the misery of Old 84, it isn't surprising that several escape attempts occurred. On November 23, 1893, three inmates obtained cutting tools from an unnamed source, cut through prison bars, and swam across the Mare Island Strait to Vallejo. They were eventually found in Canada.

In 1920, six inmates overpowered marine guards, stole their weapons, and headed to Sacramento. Twenty-five marines gave chase and found the men in Cordelia, only ten miles from Mare Island. A gunfight ensued in which two marines were wounded. The escapees were returned to Old 84 and their sentences doubled. Several escapes occurred during the World War II years, with the last one on record taking place in 1945.

During my time inside Old 84, I sensed the presence of several angry, miserable spirits. One spirit seemed to have a different demeanor. This may have been the ghost of Marine Corps Captain Arthur Matthews, warden of the prison. In 1911, Captain Matthews realized that he could open the prison safe, remove $3,100, stuff it in a bag, and walk out without comment or action by men under his command. Matthews wisely headed to Florida but soon realized that the romantic notion of joining

Pancho Villa's Mexican revolutionaries was not the adventure he desired. Deserting his comrades, he traveled to Florida, where the shame of his criminal behavior caught up to him. Being the son of a Navy admiral, the marine captain probably realized that he had betrayed the trust of the Marine Corps and tarnished the family name. Arthur decided to inflict self punishment by killing himself instead of facing the possibility of serving a long sentence in a prison he once commanded. It is likely that his ghost has returned to the prison he once commanded to make restitution and restore his good name.

OTHER PLACES TO SEARCH FOR GHOSTS ON MARE ISLAND

Murder Site
500 Block of Walnut Avenue

Many people in Vallejo will volunteer that a lot of strange things happen on Mare Island. Aside from ghosts and creepy buildings, crime happens on the island that sometimes leaves locals shaken. On May 27, 2024, the body of a dead woman was found on Walnut Street. Homicide inspectors believe that the woman was murdered at another location and then dumped at the edge of the street. The identity of the deceased has not been made public, and no arrests have been made. Ghost hunters who specialize in crime scene investigation have not obtained any paranormal evidence that may contribute to the police investigation, which is currently "cold."

Mystery Lights
Shell Mound
James Capoot Street

Archaeological research spanning the entire twentieth century has identified more than four hundred shell mounds around the San Francisco Bay Area, including two on Mare Island. Shell mounds began as early as 1000 BC when forerunners of the Ohlone tribe came upon the bay shallows, which offered them food, shelter, building materials, and a pleasant climate. Harvests of shellfish and other hunter-gatherer sustenance activities led to huge accumulations of bones, shells, human waste, tools, weapons, and other refuse. Composed mostly of shells from the bay, these dumps grew to massive proportions. Some that have been investigated by archaeologists measure more than sixty feet high, four hundred feet long, and two hundred feet wide. Over the centuries, the mounds were compacted, mixed with soil and sand brought by seasonal floods, and covered with grasses. Some Native tribes used their shell mounds as burial sites, mixing the bones of ancestors with other remnants of human occupation. It is unknown how many modern structures on Bay Area islands and surrounding communities rest on the graves of Indigenous people.

Ghost hunters who are familiar with the prehistory of the Bay Area often receive reports of paranormal activity at shell mound sites that may be attributed to disturbed spirits of Indigenous people who guard their remains or those of ancestors. A portion of the Bay Street Shopping Center in the bayside community of Emeryville sits on the remnants of a huge shell mound that may harbor protective spirits. Security staff who work at night have had plenty to say about restless spirits. Speaking on the condition of anonymity, two guards told me of human-shaped shadows and soft clouds of white light that are frequently spotted at the southeast end of the mall near the theater. Neither phenomena can be explained as merely lights from passing cars or people visiting the mall after all stores have closed. The shadows resemble people of short stature, less than five feet tall, and move with an irregular gait.

With the rapid development of shipyard facilities on Mare Island between 1870 and 1920, and again during the World War II years, shell mounds on Mare Island have essentially been obliterated, but remnants may still be found west of the old Marine Barracks. Access from the end of James Capoot Street is difficult, but adventurous ghost hunters have spotted unexplained lights hovering over a site believed to be shell mound located about 650 yards southwest of the old Marine Barracks. Remnants of a second shell mound are located at the south end of Mare Island (38.070241, -122.261174). Hiking trails to the site may be accessed from Tyler Road.

CHAPTER 6
OTHER BAY AREA LOCATIONS

Several historic sites around the north Bay Area have strong links to the haunted islands. Bar, brothels, piers, bridges, and historic vessels form a fascinating collection of venues haunted by ghosts with strong ties to the islands. Some of those ghosts lived on Mare Island, Yerba Buena, Alameda, or Angel Island or traveled to the island daily for work. Others navigated the bay on ships and sailboats by using the strong winds blowing through the Golden Gate and chaotic currents swirling about Alcatraz and Angel Island. Easy access to these mainland places provides ghost hunters with an opportunity get in touch with the history of people who lived their lives on San Francisco Bay's haunted islands.

PHANTOM SHIPS ON THE BAY

Astute ghost hunters who keep a sharp eye on San Francisco Bay when touring waterfront areas occasionally spot phantom vessels gliding under the Golden Gate Bridge, entering Ayala Cove on Angel Island, or approaching an old wharf. It is estimated that more than three hundred shipwrecks lie beneath the waters of the bay. The remains of some of these ships, hidden by the shifting sands of beaches and ebb and flow of mudflats, are sometimes exposed by fast tides. More often, phantoms of many ill-fated vessels show up on foggy nights or afternoons when the bay area's heavy overcast skies block out the horizon and seem to touch the surface of the bay's waters.

The most famous sighting of a phantom ship was made by the crew of the destroyer USS *Kennison* (DD-138). This World War II fighting ship entered fog-bound San Francisco Bay on the morning of September 15, 1942. Lookout Howard H. Brisbane alerted officers on the bridge to a large ship that lay ahead. As the fog thinned, several of the *Kennison*'s crew were astounded to see a square-rigged ship, unpainted and heavily worn by years at sea. The event was recorded in the *Kennison*'s log and widely accepted as a true account given the fact that the crew's skills in identifying ships, friend or foe, were sharpened by a long patrol in the Pacific Ocean.

The ship's battle-hardened crew spotted was the USS *Tennessee*, which sank in 1853 as it fought the treacherous currents of the Golden Gate. The rudder of the ship—which was laden with 550 passengers, 40 crew, and fourteen chests of gold bullion—failed as wind and current forced it onto the rocks at Fort Point. All souls abroad were saved and the gold salvaged, but the huge ship was a total loss. As the captain left the vessel, it slid into the depths, only to be carried away to some unknown resting spot inside the bay.

Weeks after the tragedy, people strolling the beaches of the Presidio spotted the vessel on foggy evenings. Its ragged sails and rotted timbers were in sharp contrast to the fine sailing ships arriving from the East Coast and Europe. Vessels that leave San Francisco Bay at night under foggy conditions report sighting the *Tennessee* under the Golden Gate Bridge, perhaps as a warning to beware of the treacherous currents.

The last reported sighting of the *Tennessee* was in September 2024, when a rare weather event brought wind and rain to the Bay Area. Joggers and walkers along the Presidio bike path spotted the ragged vessel as its image faded in and out with the billowing fog. Some witnesses reported hearing screams of passengers and shouts of crew.

In the early hours of the morning, when the sun's light barely penetrates the heavy overcast that blankets San Francisco's Embarcadero, the complete but transparent image of the Norwegian ship *Squando* may be spotted as it drifts from Pier 7 southward past the Ferry Building before disappearing. Paranormal investigators speculate that this phantom vessel appears because of intense negative energy arising from the ship's reputation as a venue for murder.

In 1890, Captain Nels Erickson docked the *Squando* at Pier 7 and sent the crew ashore with the exception of first mate Lars Gunderson. The captain then coerced his philandering wife into pouring several drinks for Lars with the intention of getting him drunk. When the unfortunate man was in an alcoholic stupor, the captain cut off his head as punishment for having an affair with his wife. Legend says that the headless body was dumped into the bay, while the head was kept in a bucket, perhaps as a warning to the adulterous wife.

When the headless body was discovered floating past the Ferry Building, police pursued the murderous captain and his accomplice. Some versions of the story suggest that the pair escaped to Norway, while others suggest the couple were hanged by vigilantes.

Soon after a new captain took command, he was murdered by a mutinous crew. His replacement was found dead in his bunk, while another captain's lifeless body was found slumped in his cabin chair.

Finally, the *Squando* was sailed to New Brunswick, Canada. Its horrific reputation as a cursed ship preceded its arrival, and guards refused to stay overnight on the ship after sighting a headless apparition walking the deck near the captain's cabin. As the history of this ship became widely known, the curse was not attributed to the murder of a first mate and three captains. It seems that during construction of the vessel, several men were killed by accident. The widow of one of the men cursed the ship and all who would sail on it. To seal the deal, the grieving widow killed herself. Unable to secure a crew for the ship, owners eventually demolished it and sold the hardware.

Other locations where phantom vessels have been spotted include a sinking sailboat near Alcatraz and an anchored two-masted sailing vessel off Crown Beach in Alameda. Vague images of Indian canoes have been spotted in Richardson Bay near Sausalito.

HEINOLD'S FIRST AND LAST CHANCE SALOON

48 Webster Street
Jack London Square
Oakland
510-839-6761
www.heinoldsfirstandlastchance.com

In the 1880s, the Oakland waterfront was a wild place. Ships came to call from all over the world. Their crews would hit the town with money in their pockets and lust in their hearts. Ships were often abandoned by their officers and crew, leaving the docks congested with derelict vessels that were

Heinold's First and Last Chance Saloon has been in business since 1884.

scavenged by crews of other ships who might need additional hardware, ropes, sails, or wood for fuel. In addition to crowds of sailors, the docks were full of longshoremen and naval personnel who supported a bustling community of bars and brothels and kept the jail full.

In 1879, the crew of a whaling ship was incarcerated for several weeks, leaving their ship unattended. The old vessel grounded on the Oakland mud, and soon local scavengers stripped it of wood, metal, and other valuable building materials. Much of its timber was used to build a solid structure that served three years as a boardinghouse for sailors.

In 1883, the place was purchased by Johnny Heinold for $100 and transformed into a bar. Johnny's bar became a popular waterfront gathering place for oyster pirates and the lawmen who pursued them on San Francisco Bay. The curious name—the First and Last Chance Saloon—was derived from the bar's location. The place stood at the foot of a pier from which ferryboats carried passengers across the Oakland Estuary to the dry town of Alameda. Johnny's bar was the last chance for a drink before passengers departed for Alameda and their first chance upon returning to Oakland.

In 1886, a boy named Jack London sat on the stool selling newspapers to the bar's patrons. Later, he sat at a corner table to do his schoolwork. Not only was young Jack London inspired by the exciting stories of adventure told by the men drinking at the bar, but at the age of sixteen, Jack also made a deal to purchase his first sailboat while seated at a corner table.

Over the years, sailors, soldiers, marines, aviators, and others embarking on far reaching adventures have made Heinold's bar a last stop before departure and a first stop upon returning home. Many of these adventurers have returned only in spirit. The warped floorboards, century-old chairs, stools, and tables offer an atmosphere of timelessness that is comforting to the living as well as the dead. Some ghost hunters have sensed the spirit of Jack London and members of this oyster pirate gang. Others have experienced the touch of the long-departed Johnny Heinold. Several cold spots in the tiny bar could be the spirits of famous visitors from decades past, including Robert Louis Stevenson, Earle Gardner, Ambrose Bierce, Robert Service, and Joaquin Miller. The old photographs and other maritime souvenirs mounted on the walls document the history of this old bar and provide hints of the identity of the many spirits that still visit the First and Last Chance Saloon.

REDHEADED GHOST

Captain Blythers Restaurant
123 First Street
Benicia
707-745-4082

Paranormal research groups have visited this landmark restaurant on Benicia's historic First Street in their quest for the ghost of Captain Samuel Blythers. The history of the Blythers family suggests that the patriarch or members of his family may haunt the place. In 1879, just a few weeks after the after construction of the present building was completed, the captain died in one of the second-floor rooms. Years later, his daughter, Julia, married Thomas McDermott in the house. Her husband may have left some environmental imprints of his agony in the place, as he recovered there from a traumatic amputation of his right leg caused by a railroad car passing over his limb. Blythers' wife, Annie, may have left imprints that sensitives detect as hauntings too. After Sam's death in 1879, she continued to live in the house as a widow, raising three children. She died in the kitchen in 1909.

Environmental imprints of the Blythers family or ghosts or Sam and Annie may be found in this popular restaurant, but staff members and patrons I spoke to believe that the most active spirit in the place in that of a redheaded prostitute. After the death of the last Blythers family member, George, the building was sold and used as a boardinghouse for a short time before it became a brothel known as the Alamo Rooms. Its location at the foot of First Street, adjacent to the train station and the riverfront docks, made it a convenient location for the kind of men who would patronize such a business. During World War II, the place was one of eleven brothels in Benicia, and business was profitable, allowing for renovation of the second floor into eight small rooms. The restaurant's manager told me that each room had a double bed, nightstand, a small window, and hooks on the wall for hanging clothing. One room had a "mayor's closet" accessed through a concealed door. It provided the mayor and other town officials a hiding place during police raids in the 1950s.

In 1982, the brothel was gutted and converted to a restaurant. Soon after the second floor was renovated as a bar, the apparition of a tall, slim, redheaded woman began to appear to staff members and customers. At first, this ghost showed up near closing time, leading most witnesses to dismiss the experience as the effects of fatigue and alcohol. But staff members working during the day noticed that objects were moved in inexplicable ways. Glass, ash trays, chairs, barstools, and napkins were either lined up in orderly fashion or scattered, depending on how staff members had left them. Some workers reported feeling as though someone stood close to them or touched them as they worked alone in the building.

Eventually, the redheaded ghost appeared so frequently that staff named her Rebecca. Naturally, there is no record available of the brothel's employees or owner, but a psychic who visited the place in 2008 without prior knowledge of its history told me that she detected the presence of a woman named Reba, a nickname for Rebecca. The psychic also noted the Reba is happy with the place, especially because the customers are cleaner than her former patrons and she doesn't have to share a bed with them.

GHOSTS OF THE CHINESE FISHERMEN

China Camp Regional Park
North San Pedro Road
San Rafael
415-456-0766

During the 1860s, thousands of Chinese laborers were imported to California to build the Union Pacific Railroad, construct mines and tunnels, and work in industries such as brick manufacture and mining. After a few years of working dangerous jobs under harsh conditions, Chinese who had worked as fishermen in China abandoned their occupations and established thirty shrimping villages around the San Francisco Bay. At McNear's Point in modern-day Marin County, the village was initially composed of renegade fishermen who had escaped from contracts that would have kept them working for decades. Their dwellings were so crude that the place became known as China Camp. Early success brought modest wealth, enabling the fishermen to establish families. At its height, China Camp was home for seventy-seven fishermen who supported more than five hundred people. In the early days of the shrimp industry, few laws regulated business. In 1901, 1905, and 1911, laws were enacted that made Chinese fishing methods illegal or severely limited the tonnage that could be taken from the bay. As a result, many fishermen operated outside the law.

Earlier illegal activities of shrimp fishermen served as basis of several stories by famed local author Jack London. In his *Tales of the Fish Patrol* and the classic short stories "Yellow Handkerchief" and "Yellow and White," London describes his exploits against the fishermen of China Camp as a member of the fish patrol (forerunner of the state fish and game wardens). Early in the twentieth century, encounters between Chinese fishermen and law enforcement officers were often violent. Some shrimpers were shot or drowned. Other tragedies that befell this community included fires that almost destroyed the village and the great earthquake of 1906.

Some of the residents of old China Camp who lost their lives more than a century ago still occupy the place. While sitting on the quiet beach, visitors have heard Chinese spoken in muffled tones. This audio phenomenon has been captured on tape and other recording media by ghost hunters. At

The structures at China Camp Regional Park retain the paranormal imprints of a nineteenth-century community of fishermen.

places where the remains of shacks are found, cold spots occur and light anomalies show up in photographs.

Buildings currently standing at the camp are reproductions, but they were constructed from boards and timbers found at the site that were once part of the Chinese community. Consequently, sensitives who visit the shacks and pier get bizarre impressions that include the sound of chimes, flutes, and drums; odors of rotting fish; and the shuffle of feet on the ground. One of the best sightings at China Camp was a vision of a Chinese fishing boat that appeared a short distance offshore. The boat was estimated to be forty feet long with a single large sail typical of Chinese junks. Six to eight men were seen on deck as the boat glided into the shallows with its sail slack. Upon coming to a stop, the boat vanished.

GOLDEN GATE BRIDGE

San Francisco
415-921-5858

On August 5, 1775, Juan de Ayala became the first European to sail through the narrow entrance to San Francisco Bay that would later be known as the Golden Gate. For the next seventy-five years, the 1.25-mile-wide channel remained an elusive target for ships' navigators, resulting in many wrecks. Soon after the Americans took California from the Mexicans in 1846, travel across the Golden Gate between San Francisco and settlements in Marin County by small boats and rafts became frequent but proved dangerous as swift tides and strong winds caused many drownings. In the early part of the twentieth century, ferryboats carried large numbers of passengers between Sausalito, Tiburon, San Rafael, and San Francisco. Sometime in the late 1920s, the idea that a bridge could span the gap was introduced.

The Golden Gate Bridge project began in 1932 with construction of two huge towers that stood about 1.1 miles apart. During construction of the foundations for these towers, at least three workers fell into the flowing wet cement, to be buried alive and forever entombed in the base of the Golden Gate Bridge.

Soon after the bridge opened, it became a popular place for committing suicide. Since 1936, more than 1,200 people have hopped the railing and thrown themselves to their deaths. It is widely believed that the actual number of suicides is much greater. The drop from mid-span to the water's surface is 286 feet. From that height, the velocity on impact is so great that the effect on a human body is the same as hitting concrete. Ghost hunters who seek spirits on the Golden Gate should view a documentary film by Eric Steel titled *The Bridge*. In 2004, Steel's cameras captured the images of nineteen people as they jumped to their deaths from the span.

FORT POINT

**Long Avenue at Marine Drive
San Francisco, CA 94129
415-556-1693
www.nps.gov**

Standing in the shadow of the Golden Gate Bridge, this lonely remnant of a distant historical period possesses an intense ghostly atmosphere. Cold, dark, brick corridors, bastions, and casemates still fitted with massive cannons offer quick passage to another time, putting the sensitive visitor in touch with spirits that still stand guard on the ramparts or practice gunnery.

The first fort on this site was a crude adobe and log facility constructed by Spanish soldiers in 1794. By 1821, the tiny fort had fallen into disrepair from neglect and the harsh San Francisco climate. This decaying outpost served little purpose until 1846, when it became a military objective of the Bear Flag revolt. Kit Carson led a group of Americans across the Golden Gate and up the sandy slope to attack the poorly manned fort. Later, the strategic importance of the site was recognized by the U.S. Army, especially with the onset of the California Gold Rush in 1849 and the massive influx of foreign ships into the Bay Area.

Construction of the present fort was begun in 1853 and completed in 1861 with the assistance of army engineer Robert E. Lee. As the largest masonry fort west of the Mississippi River, Fort Point has been called the "Gibraltar of the West" and "one of the most perfect models of masonry in America." Together with gun emplacements on Alcatraz and at Fort Lime Point near the present town of Sausalito, Fort Point was America's primary means of defending San Francisco and Northern California from foreign encroachment. Despite its extensive armament, Fort Point never fired a gun in battle. Instead, the lonely fort had slipped into disrepair and decay by the turn of the century. Fortuitous circumstances saved the fort from destruction when the Golden Gate Bridge was constructed in the 1930s. After extensive renovation, the essence of an era has been revived.

As visitors to Fort Point pass down the dark, deserted corridors, the sounds of soldiers living on the very frontier of America, far from home, mix with the roar of surf surging against the outer walls. Many soldiers came to this desolate place with a sense of apprehension over the harshness of life and duty at the fort and a longing to return to civilized America. Some lost their

Fort Point guarded the entrance to the bay, dubbed the Golden Gate, since 1861, many years before the bridge was constructed.

dreams amid the tumultuous history of the opening of the West to never return to the East or Midwest. A few of these lost soldiers still stand guard at Fort Point on the Golden Gate. One of them, Private James Aitchison, died at the fort on January 5, 1965, of mysterious cause. His ghost is said to walk the barracks of the second floor. Other ghosts of soldiers who died during the bubonic plague epidemic of 1900 walk these rooms too. During the four years of plague infestation, hundreds of soldiers were quarantined in the fort, and an unknown number died there.

Outside the walls of the fort, sensitives often detected the tortured souls of passengers who died on February 21, 1901, when the SS *City of Rio de Janeiro* crashed into the rocks. Reportedly, panic swept the decks as passengers fought for the inadequate supply of life jackets and seats in leaky lifeboats. Witnesses reported that most of the lifeboats, launched less than one hundred yards from shore, sank, spilling passengers into the icy water. Less than thirty minutes after striking the rocks, 129 passengers and crew died in the waters off Fort Point, while only 85 survived. Many who made it ashore clung to the rocks as waves washed over them. Their screams for help can be heard by sensitives and sometimes captured on audio recorders.

GHOSTS OF THE *BALCLUTHA*'S SAILORS

Mare Island Naval Shipyards
Coal Sheds
850 Nimitz Avenue
www.nps.gov

This tall, beautiful, square-rigged ship was built in Glasgow, Scotland, and launched in 1886. More than 300 feet in length, its three masts rise 145 feet above the deck, giving her a sleek and majestic appearance. It served for many years by hauling coal from England to San Francisco. On the return voyage to England, it carried grain from the San Joaquin Valley loaded at San Francisco wharves. These ten-thousand-mile voyages took it through tropical heat, freezing cold, and many storms, as well as the treacherous Cape Horn, which it rounded seventeen times in a thirteen-year period.

As with many sailing vessels of its day, men died on board. Healthcare was nonexistent, and the splinting of broken bones and stitching of lacerations was often left to the cook or sail maker. Several sailors died of chronic illnesses such as diabetes and lung disease, while others succumbed to hard labor. Virtually every sailor who died on board was buried at sea. The early logbooks of the *Balclutha* are not available to determine how many at-sea burials took place, but records from similar ships suggest at least five deaths per year. Whatever the number of deaths that occurred on the *Balclutha*, it appears that several decided to stay abroad after their bodies were committed to the deep.

This huge sailing vessel is a spooky ship, especially below decks when no one is around. Visitors have been so surprised by eerie sounds that they've made reports to docents that must be described as paranormal. Below decks, odd sounds are heard that include the muted moaning sailors struggling through their final minutes of life. Unexplained sounds also include coughing, whistling, flute, drums, and the shuffling of boot-clad feet on the deck. Sometimes, visitors feel the cold presence of someone standing behind them or cold spots near the crew's quarters. An intense cold spot is often detected near the foremast on the starboard side of the ship. This may be the spot where a sailor landed after falling from the tall mast during a gale off Cape Horn.

While ghost hunters visit the *Balclutha*, they should take note of the vessel's characteristics, including the shape of the hull, sweep of the decks,

The nineteenth-century sailing ship *Balclutha* retains its ghostly crew after having been moved to Mare Island.

and position of yardarms on the mast. Familiarity with these features may enable ghost hunters to spot ghosts ships floating on San Francisco Bay that resemble the *Balclutha*. On foggy days, visitors to the waterfront have been astonished to glimpse the sight of a tall, square-rigged ship gliding out of the mist only to disappear again. Some have called the police or Coast Guard to report that the *Balclutha* has slipped its moorings and drifted into the shipping lanes on the bay. Panicked callers are reassured that the great ship is safely moored. What these people saw is one of several ghost ships from the nineteenth century that still sail the bay. The most famous sighting occurred on September 15, 1942, when the destroyer USS *Kennison* entered the fog-bound bay. Fresh from combat in the Pacific, the ship's lookout, Howard H. Brisbane, called the bridge to report an old sailing vessel with two masts that came into sight as the fog lifted. Brisbane entered his report into the *Kennison*'s log, which included mention of two masts, an unpainted hull, and ragged sails. Several crew members came on deck to get a look at the old ship as the *Kennison* maneuvered to avoid collision. After the two vessels passed each other, the sailing ship disappeared in a fog.

This sighting is considered one of the most valid ever made because the *Kennison*'s crew were fresh from combat and their skills in observing other vessels were considered highly developed and not prone to error. Added to that, at least thirty men on board the destroyer witnessed the older vessel.

USS *Pampanito* (SS-383)

Pier, Fisherman's Wharf
Taylor and Embarcadero Streets
San Francisco, CA 94133
415-775-1943

As one of the most popular historic vessels in the United States, this World War II submarine hosts eleven thousand visitors each year and offers several overnight experiences. Fully restored to 1945 operational standards, the sub takes sensitive visitors back more than sixty years. The ambience of this fighting boat includes a few spots where paranormal activity has been detected. The forward torpedo room, engine room, and conning tower may be hot spots for residuals or environmental imprints.

There are few documented reports of ghostly activity on this submarine because investigation is virtually impossible. Access is limited to hours when the sub is open to visitors. At any given time, there may be thirty people inside the cramped quarters. The best time to seek ghosts in this historic vessel is the final fifteen minute before closing.

USS *Potomac* (AG-25)

Presidential Yacht
540 Water Street
Jack London Square
Oakland 94604-2064
510-627-1215

This stately vessel was built in 1934 to serve as a Coast Guard cutter and was christened the *Electra*. In 1936, ignoring the maritime curse of bad luck for any vessel that is renamed, the Navy converted the 376-ton cutter to a presidential yacht for Franklin Roosevelt and renamed it the USS *Potomac*. It had a long and glorious career as a presidential yacht without many spells of bad luck, but it did end up on the wrong side of the law at the bottom of San Francisco Bay.

The presidential yacht *Potomac* was a favored refuge from the stress of World War I for President Franklin Roosevelt and other dignitaries.

Roosevelt used the yacht to meet with his closest advisors and entertain foreign dignitaries such as King George and Queen Elizabeth of England, as well as used it as a floating venue for retreat from the summer heat of Washington, D.C. Eleanor Roosevelt celebrated her fifty-seventh birthday on the yacht in 1941. After the president's death in 1945, the USS *Potomac* passed through private hands until it was purchased by a company that fronted for drug smugglers who operated along the West Coast. In 1980, it was seized by federal agents on San Francisco Bay and its hull was pierced; it sank in the shallows of Treasure Island. Two years later, the Navy refloated it and sold the historic ship to the Port of Oakland. For several years, it sat on wood blocks in full view of people traveling on I-80 in Oakland. I recall seeing the ship's engines sitting on blocks and looking like rusted hunks of metal. Stripped to the ribs, this once proud ship appears to me to be beyond repair, yet years of work and hundreds of thousands of dollars have restored it to its former glory. The USS *Potomac* was used for cruises on the San Francisco, but it now sits as a dockside museum.

The spirits of at least three ghosts have been detected on the *Potomac*. In the engine room, sensitives have sensed a man dressed in dark clothing, no doubt a sailor who operated the machinery. He doesn't seem to move about or make gestures with his hands. He merely stands as if awaiting orders from the bridge. In the forward crew's quarters, strange sounds plus humming and muted laughter are often heard. One ghost hunter told me that she experienced a profound sense of fear and sadness there. She feels this is related to the ship's days in the drug smuggling business.

On the fantail, the pale image of a short man dressed in a suit appears near the railing. He may have been one of FDR's political advisors. Perhaps he has returned to attend the president's cocktail parties, staged there for FDR's closest friends and advisors.

CHAPTER 7
HOW TO EXPERIENCE PARANORMAL ACTIVITY

Based partly on the kind of paranormal activity reported at a site, the ghost hunter must decide which method or approach will be used. Some will feel competent with a collection of cameras, electromagnetic field detectors, digital thermometers, computers, data recorders, and other high-tech gadgets. These ghost hunters prefer to use the "technical method." Others may discover that they have an emotional affinity for a particular historic site, a surprising fascination with an event associated with a haunting, or empathy for a deceased person. These ghost hunters may have success with the "psychic method." Another consideration is the ghost hunter's goal. Some desire scientific evidence of ghostly presence, while others simply want to experience paranormal activity.

THE TECHNICAL METHOD

Professional and advanced amateur ghost hunters often use an array of detection and recording devices that cover a wide range of the electromagnetic spectrum. This approach can be complicated and expensive and require technically skilled people to operate the devices. Ghost hunters who want to keep their investigations simple may get satisfying results with common audio and video recording devices and other low-tech methods.

STILL-PHOTOGRAPHY TECHNIQUES

Many photographic techniques that work well under normal conditions are inadequate for ghost hunts. That's because ghost hunting is usually conducted under conditions of low ambient light. This requires the use of long exposures. Some investigators use a strobe or flash device, but these can make the photos look unauthentic or create artifacts.

If you use digital photographic methods, practice taking pictures under conditions of low ambient light, with and without artificial lighting. Most digital cameras have default automatic settings that might not well work during a ghost investigation. These settings may not be easily changed as ambient conditions change at the haunted site unless you have practiced the procedures. Many cameras have features that enable automatic exposures at specific intervals (e.g., once every minute). This allows a hands-off remote photograph record to be made. Repetitive automatic exposures also allow a site to be investigated without the presence of the investigator.

While every ghost hunter armed with a camera wishes to capture the full-bodied image of a ghost, most have to settle for light anomalies. These may be amorphous, luminescent clouds, narrow streaks of light resembling a shooting star. The light anomaly most frequently found in digital images is the orb. An orb is a symmetrical white disk that appears most often in photographic and digital images made under low-light conditions. It may appear hovering near a ceiling, over a bed, or inside a car. A digital image may contain a single orb or show so many of varying sizes that they cannot be counted. Impressive pictures of light anomalies may be viewed at several websites.

Many ghost hunters claim that orbs are spirit manifestations without explaining why the spirit of a human would appear as a disk of light. Some of these have a humanoid shape but fail to convince critics and skeptics that the image is that of a ghost because the image is so perfectly illuminated that it appears fake. Software for processing digital images has reduced the power of proof that was once attributed to photographs. Critics and skeptics point out that orbs may be the result of bugs, dust particles, or water droplets suspended in the air close to the lens or inside the camera. Excited ghost hunters have displayed pictures of light anomalies that turn out to be the result of wisps of hair, a camera strap, a finger, cigarette smoke, light reflected from jewelry, or smudges on the lens.

It is interesting to note that orbs were virtually unheard of in the field of paranormal investigation until digital cameras became available.

Consequently, many people suspect that orbs may be the result of operating characteristics of the camera. Under conditions of low light, pixels of a digital camera may not fill in completely. This has been called under-pixilation. As a result, no image information or electronic signal is generated. The lack of a signal is detected by the camera's software, which then fills in the missing spot in the picture's signal array with white light. The result is an orb.

Is it possible that a spirit will manifest as an orb? Yes, although many experts suggest that as many as 99 percent of orb pictures do not represent anything paranormal. I've seen some very impressive orbs, however. Ghost hunter Jackie Ganiy, president of Sonoma SPIRIT, captured a picture of an orb hovering over the flight deck of the aircraft carrier USS *Hornet* in Alameda, California. This orb was symmetrically rounded, but a skull was visible within it. Books by Melvyn Willin and Troy Taylor present fascinating collections of the best pictures of ghosts and other paranormal light anomalies, including orbs.

Generally, light anomalies should not be readily accepted as evidence of spirit manifestation unless there is corroborating evidence from other technical devices. This includes audio phenomena, changes in electromagnetic field, isolated changes in air temperature, or other still or video images. Evidence might also be found in psychic impressions experience at the time and place that the orb picture was created. Psychic impressions of intense emotions, sobbing, and cries for help or screaming might be obtained while standing in an old hospital room as a photographer captures a picture of an orb hovering over the bed.

AUDIO RECORDING TECHNIQUES

Digital recorders provide an inexpensive way to obtain audio evidence of ghostly activity. The popular term for this is electronic voice phenomena, or EVP. The American Association for EVP defines the process as any intelligible voice detected on recording media that has no known explanation. Most ghost hunters accept a wider definition, which includes the sound of moving objects, such as doors, windows, glass objects, whistling, sobbing, laughter, screams, humming, gunshots, footsteps, explosions, musical notes, or tapping and knocking. Given this wide variety of sounds, I've proposed that the term EVP be replaced by EAP, or electronic audio phenomena, defined as any audio recording that cannot be attributed to normal phenomena.

EAP are obtained as a ghost hunter operates an audio recording device while investigating an allegedly haunted place. The ghost hunter may record an EAP while remaining stationary at a site, such as next to a grave or while walking around. This is called an EAP or EVP sweep. Generally, questions are asked to which spirits may respond. These questions should be simple and follow an invitation for any spirit to communicate, even if only by a nonvocal sound. Typical questions include:

- "What is your name?"
- "Did you die here?"
- "How old are you?"
- "Do you want me to leave?
- "Why are you here?"

Your research may indicate specific questions you can use in your EAP investigations. If you seek a ghost of a prison inmate who committed suicide by hanging himself in a cell, you may ask, "Did you die in this cell?" or "Did you hang yourself?" The ghost hunter may also provoke a spirit through verbal confrontation or insult.

In most cases, spirit responses cannot be heard by the ghost hunter, but they may be discovered on the audio recording during playback. Typically, responses are brief, rarely lasting more than a few seconds. Vocalizations sometimes have amazing clarity, but most often they are unintelligible and, as with other sounds, are rarely repeated in subsequent recordings. If the spirit's response forms a clear and reasonable answer to the question, the recording may be called a "specific" EAP. Other responses, whether they are vocalizations or other sounds, must be labeled "random" EAP and scrutinized as the result of processes that are not paranormal. For example, the sound of a conversation between two living people may be carried a long distance across a body of water.

A ghost hunter who is unaware of others in the area may ask, "What is your name?" The response discovered during playback may be "I am cold." This may be a random EAP or a non-paranormal recording of words spoken by a living person. Random EAP may be created by natural or normal processes, such as the wind against a window or drafts in an old house, and there is high likelihood that they do not reflect a spirit's intelligent interaction with the investigator. Specific EAP has greater value as evidence of ghostly presence because clear and reasonable responses to specific questions are not likely to be created by random conversations among living people nearby or natural processes.

Often, EAP consists of nonvocal sounds. Musical instruments, slamming doors, gunshots, footsteps, and tapping sounds may be evoked by the ghost hunter's questions. Ghosts that are unable to generate vocalizations may resort to these sounds as the only means of communication. These may be random EAP but still comprise good evidence of a ghostly presence. You may ask, "Why are you here?" On playback, the recording may reveal the sound of footsteps moving away from the microphone. In this instance, the ghost may have been troubled by the question and decided to leave.

While EAP are seldom heard through the human auditory sense, they may be captured on recording media by one of two ways. Spirits may encode their intention or effort to create sound telepathically onto the magnetic tape or electronics of the recording device by manipulation of its internal electromagnetic fields. Or a vocalization, musical note, or other sound that was previously imprinted on the electromagnetic field of the environment may be triggered to "play" by the ghost hunter and detected by the recording device. In the case of the latter, the EAP is typically random, suggesting that no spirit is present, but the experience is still paranormal. Ghost hunters who have exceptional luck in acquiring paranormal audio recordings have been called "EVP magnets."

Before you begin your EAP sweep, test your recorder under conditions you expect to find at the investigation site in order to reduce audio artifact and ensure optimal performance of the device. Does your recorder pick up excessive background noise? This may obscure ghostly sounds. If so, consider upgrading the tape quality or selecting a high-quality digital audio recorder. Consider using a wind guard on the microphone.

Consider using two or more recorders at different locations within the site. This allows you to verify sounds such as wind against a window and reduce the possibility of ambiguous recordings or misinterpretation of an EAP.

Allow time, at least fifteen to sixty seconds, for a response. EAP can be heard only during playback, so ghost hunters should review recordings every five to ten minutes rather than waiting until the investigation is completed. This will enable the identification of hot spots for spirit activity that may be investigated more thoroughly.

You can use sound-activated recorders at a site overnight. They will automatically switch on whenever a sound occurs above a minimum threshold. Be aware that tape recorders may yield recordings that start with an annoying artifact, the result of a slow tape speed, at the beginning of each recorded segment. The slow tape speed could obscure the sounds made by a ghost.

Remote microphones and monitor earphones allow you to remain some distance from the site and activate the recorder when ghostly sounds are heard. If this equipment is not available, use long-play modes (sixty to ninety minutes or more), turn the recorder on, and let it run throughout your investigation, whether you remain stationary or walk about the site.

Wear a lapel microphone connected to a small audio recorder carried in your pocket. Operated in the sound-activation mode, this device will also provide you with a means of making audio notes rather than written notes. A headset with a microphone is especially useful with this technique.

Ghost hunters must carefully analyze their audio recordings, and the environment in which they are obtained, to be certain they are not inadvertent recordings of natural or normal sounds. Sound may carry great distances, particularly over bodies of water and when there is fog or low overcast skies. If a tape recorder is used, a new tape may reduce the chances of artifact. I recommend computer software such as Adobe Audition for editing your EAP recording. With a little practice, you will be able to suppress or eliminate extraneous sounds while enhancing spirit communications.

The American Association for EVP maintains a website for general information and advice (www.AA-EVP.com). Several websites may be accessed to hear examples of EVP. Use a search engine aimed at "EVP" to locate them.

VIDEO RECORDING

Video recorders offer a wide variety of recording features from time-lapse to auto-start/stop and auto focus. These features enable you to make surveillance-type recordings over many hours while you are off-site. Consult your user's manual for low-light recording guidelines and always use a tripod and long-duration battery packs.

If you plan to attempt video recording, consider using two recorders at equal distance from a specific object such as a chair. Arrange the recorders at different angles, preferably ninety degrees from each other.

Another approach you might try is to use a wide-angle setting on the first camera to get a broad view of a room, porch, or courtyard. On the second camera, use a close-up setting to capture ghostly apparitions at a door, chair, or window.

You may have more success with sequential, manual, or timer-actuated recordings than a continuous-run technique. If you try this technique, use recording runs of one to five minutes. Practice using the method that interrupts the automatic setting should you need to manually control the recording process. Always use a tripod that can be moved to a new location in a hurry.

HIGH-TECH EQUIPMENT

You can buy devices such as electromagnetic field detectors, infrared thermometers, barometers, and motion detectors at your local electronics store or over the Internet. Good sources for high-tech ghost hunting equipment are the Society for Paranormal Investigation, the Ghost Hunter Store, and the EMF Safety Superstore.

Inexpensive, battery-operated motion detectors can be placed at several locations within an investigation site. Some of these allow users to select an audio signal or a silent flashing light signal and connect the output to a central monitor. These devices work by measuring optical or acoustical changes in the environment. Therefore, they are most reliable when remote surveillance is performed and investigators are certain that no living beings have entered the site.

Infrared thermometers have been used to search for cold spots that may signal the presence of a ghost. While these devices are widely used and sometimes displayed on paranormal TV shows, they are often used incorrectly. They cannot be used to assess changes in the temperature of an air mass because of its very low density and minimal emission of IR energy. Infrared thermometers may be used to detect the surface temperature of solid objects, liquids, dense gases, and clouds. With a laser to assist aiming, the device can be used to measure the temperature of objects that cannot be reached due to obstructions such as fences and hazards such bodies of water that cannot be crossed, unsafe structures, or animals.

Night-vision goggles can be useful in low-light situations. These devices enhance the intensity of light within the visual spectrum and augment the resulting image with non-visual sources of electromagnetic radiation such as near infrared or ultraviolet light. Night-vision devices enable users to see doors and other objects move that you might not otherwise see. The resulting scene appears monochromatic but preserves fine details.

The most advanced and expensive piece of equipment used by ghost hunters is the FLIR imaging device. This acronym stands for "forward-looking infrared." FLIRs detect thermal energy in the infrared range.

The FLIR lens focuses the scene on a vast array of sensors that produce thousands of simultaneous measurements of thermal energy. Software then assembles the thermal measurements into a mosaic or picture that is displayed on a hand-held video screen. In the picture, elements of the scene are colored according to the temperature or level of infrared radiation. The result resembles a coloring-book image in which some elements are blue, indicating colder temperatures, while others are yellow, orange, or red, indicating warmer temperatures.

FLIR systems can see through atmospheric obscurants such as smoke or fog and in total darkness. Ghost hunters use them to detect spirits that do not generate an image within the human visual spectrum. Theoretically, when spirits appear on our plane, they draw energy from the environment, creating a cold spot. A FLIR will detect subtle changes in temperature and depict the shape of the cold spot on the video screen. When the shape of the cold spot is humanoid, ghost hunters claim that they have evidence that a ghost is present.

Despite the technical sophistication and expense of FLIRs, the images they produce may be misinterpreted. FLIRs may detect sources of heat or cold created by normal processes not noticed by the user. A living being who occupied the scene moments before a FLIR-equipped ghost hunter arrived may leave residual heat in a chair or on a doorknob. Finding the scene unoccupied by any living being, the ghost hunter might mistakenly cite the detected thermal anomaly as evidence of ghostly presence.

Electromagnetic field (EMF) detectors are used by paranormal investigators to detect the presence of ghosts in spite of the lack of scientific evidence that EMF and spirit presence are linked. Ghost hunters who use EMF detectors claim that spikes in a local electromagnetic field are created when a ghost transitions onto our plane of existence. These devices, however, often pick up EMF generated by unseen electrical appliances, faulty wiring in an old house, cellphones, walkie-talkies, video recorders, and numerous other sources, including solar flares and geomagnetic storms. EMF detectors may be useful if proper controls are established and all possible sources of natural EMF are identified.

Electronic gadgets can be useful and fun, but unless you have a means of creating a record of the instrument's output or storing images or data in a computer, your reports of light anomalies, apparent paranormal motion of objects, changes in the physical characteristics of the environment, or apparitions will not constitute the kind of hard evidence you need to satisfy skeptics. Keep in mind that even expensive instruments may produce erroneous data or signals if they are incorrectly calibrated, misused, or improperly maintained. Also, data can be easily misinterpreted if the user does not understand the technical or operating limitations of the device. The use of expensive high-tech gadgets does not guarantee accurate results, nor does it validate a ghost hunt as scientific investigation.

LOW-TECH DEVICES

I've had great success in detecting spirit activity with common household items that comprise a low-tech method of investigating the paranormal. Ghosts often become active when they are irritated by changes in their favored environment. If you tilt a picture hanging on the wall, leave an object in the ghost's rocking chair, or leave a book open, a ghost may straighten the picture, remove the object from his chair, or close the book.

Spirits may be attracted to objects they can manipulate easily. Leave four aces at the top of a deck of cards. A ghost may shuffle them throughout the deck. Ghosts are often attracted to water. A glass left full may later be found empty and the contents wetting the floor. A paper and pencil may be used by a ghost to leave bizarre marks or a legible message. Place two stacks of coins—ten pennies in each stack—on a stable surface and leave the room for an extended period of time. When you return, the coins may be scattered. If both stacks are scattered, a gust of wind or vibration of the building may account for the change. If one stack remains untouched while the other is scattered, that may be the work of a ghost. I used this technique at the Myrtles Plantation in Saint Francisville, Louisiana. I found ten pennies rearranged in a circle around the other stack of coins, which remained standing.

THE PSYCHIC METHOD

The "psychic method" relies on your intuition, inner vision, or emotional connection with a deceased person, object, place, or point of time in history. You don't have to be a trained psychic to use this approach. All of us have some capacity to tap into unseen dimensions and use some of the psychic tools described in the parapsychology literature and popular books by authors such as Sylvia Brown and Jane Roberts. Your ability to use psychic tools for successful ghost hunting depends on three factors: innate ability, receptivity, and sensitivity.

You may have an ability to successfully use psychic tools in a ghost hunt if you are one of those people who can readily identify isolated places within a room that give that chilling feeling that there is something bizarre or paranormal about the spot. The ability to identify these places must include a capacity to sort out your impressions, clear your mind of extraneous thoughts and distractions, and focus your attention on the particular point from which a paranormal impression emanates.

Your may have sufficient receptivity to effectively use psychic tools if you feel more intensely connected to a place or past era than others or often feel mentally transported to another era. Do you often get that curious feeling that some unseen person is standing behind you, watching you, or touching you? When you touch an artifact, such as a weapon, do you get the impression that you have become aware of information about the object or its user? If so, you are receptive to unseen dimensions and likely to have success hunting ghost with psychic tools. Highly receptive people often visit a place for the first time yet feel they have been there before. This is called ESP, or extrasensory perception, and reflects a high degree of receptivity.

Your receptivity can provide considerable focus to your ghost hunt if you first obtain information about the key elements and historical context of the entity's death. This includes architectural elements of a home, theater, airplane, or ship and objects such as furniture, clothing, weapons, or any implement or artifact of the specific time period of the entity's death. Touching or handling pertinent artifacts, sitting in the deceased person's chair, or standing within the historic site will enable you to get in touch with the historical moment that is most pertinent to the ghost.

You may have exceptional sensitivity if you get vivid impressions of emotions in specific locations within allegedly haunted places. Do you walk into a historic building and get that eerie feeling that something or someone from the past still lingers there? Do you get a sense of fear, anger, pain, or suffering when you visit historic places or places known to be haunted? If so, you may be sensitive to residual energies from past events, emotions that played out in a particular place, or the actions of people who have been gone from the scene for decades. Sensitive people often detect a distant time, voice, sound, touch, or texture of another dimension often described as a change in atmosphere.

Your sensitivity will pay off in a ghost hunt if your investigation is aimed at strong paranormal imprints or attachments of spirits. Strong imprints and attachments are indicated by the frequency, duration, and consistency of the paranormal event reported to occur at a particular place. The strongest imprints are created by intense emotions such as fear, rage, jealously, revenge, or loss, especially if they were repetitive over long periods of time prior to death. Strong attachments are created by love for a person, a place, or an object or a sense of obligation to provide guidance and protection. Biographical research may reveal this kind of information, particularly if personal letters or diaries are examined. Old newspaper articles, suicide notes, and photographs are useful too.

You may enhance your sensitivity by developing and expressing empathy for the ghost's lingering presence at a haunted site. Empathy can be based on your research, which may reveal information about the entity's personal history and probable emotions, motivations, problems, or unfinished business at the time of death. You may also learn that a ghost may be trapped, confused, or have chosen to remain at a site to protect someone or guard something precious. Historical sources like newspaper articles and obituaries, old photographs, or biographies can help you discern the motivations behind a ghost's reluctance to move on. Useful, intimate details might be found in letters, suicide notes, diaries, and wills.

Your sensitivity to ghostly environmental imprints and spirit manifestations may also be increased by meditation, the relaxing one's physical body to eliminate distracting thoughts and tensions and achieve emotional focus. Meditation allows you to focus your spiritual awareness on a single subject—a place, entity, or historic moment in time. As the subject comes into focus, you can add information obtained from your research such as the type of device used for a suicide or murder, favored book, musical instrument, and more. Through this process, you will become aware of unseen dimensions of the world around you, creating a feeling that you have moved through time to a distant era. Meditation gets you in touch with the place, date, and time pertinent to a ghost's imprint or death. It also enables you to disregard personal concerns and distracting thoughts that may interfere with your concentration on the ghost you seek.

Keep in mind that it is possible to be in a meditative state while appearing quite normal. The process is simple and easy to learn. When you arrive at the site of your ghost hunt, find a place a short distance away to meditate. Three essentials for any effective meditation are comfort, quiet, and concentration:

- COMFORT: Sit or stand in a relaxed position. Take free and even breaths at a slow rate. Do not alter your breathing pattern so much that you feel short of breath, winded, or lightheaded. Close your eyes if that enhances your comfort or focus on a candle, a tree, or a flower. Do not fall asleep. Proper meditation creates relaxation without decreasing alertness.

- Quiet: Meditate in a place away from noises generated by traffic, passersby, radios, slammed doors, and the like. If you are with a group, give others sufficient personal space. Some people use mantras, repetitive words or phrases, or speak only in their mind in order to facilitate inner calmness. Mantras are useful to induce a focused state of relaxation, but they may disrupt the meditation of a companion if spoken aloud. A majority of ghost hunters do not believe that mantras are necessary in this instance. They point out that ghost hunting is not like a séance as depicted in movies. It is not necessary to chant special words, call out to the dead, or invite an appearance "from beyond the grave."
- Concentration: First, clear your mind of everyday thoughts, worries, and concerns. This is the most difficult part of the process. Many of us don't want to let go of our stressful thoughts. To help you let go of those thoughts, let the thought turn off its light and fade into darkness. After you clear your mind, some thoughts may reappear. Repeat the process. Slowly turn off the light of each thought until you can rest with a completely cleared mind. This might take some practice. Don't wait until you are on the scene of a ghost hunt before you practice this exercise.

Once your mind is clear, focus on your breathing and imagine your entire being as a single point of energy driving the breathing process. Then, open yourself. Think only of the entity you seek. Starting with the ghost's identity (if known), slowly expand your focus to include its personal history, the historical era of the ghost's death or creation of the emotional imprint, the reported nature and appearance of the haunting, and any specific ghostly activity.

Acknowledge each thought as you continue relaxed breathing. Find a thought that is most attractive to you and then expand your mind to include your present surroundings. Return slowly to your current place and time. Remain quiet for a minute or two before you resume communication with your companions and then move ahead with the ghost hunt.

PSYCHIC TOOLS

Clairaudience: Impression of sounds generated by paranormal sources may be perceived through clairaudience. The term is derived from the French, meaning clear hearing. People with this ability may hear the voices of spirits that are trying to communicate or sounds of events that occurred years or decades earlier. The latter are environmental imprints most often created by intense repetitive emotions or events that had a strong emotional component.

Clairsentience: Some ghosts manifest by creating impressions of physical sensations in receptive people that may include a feeling of being touched and perception of fragrances or odors. The ability to perceive or detect impressions of physical sensations that do not truly exist in real time is called clairsentience. Signature perfumes or the fragrance of favorite flowers can help you identify a ghost. At the world-renowned haunted Myrtles Plantation in Louisiana, the ghost of Sarah Woodruff creates the fragrance of her favorite flower, the magnolia. Odors such as cigars, oranges, and hemp are common ghostly manifestations. Sometimes ghost hunters encounter the noxious odors of rotting meat or burning flesh.

Clairvoyance: Information or impressions may be received from objects or spirits at the present time without the use of "normal" senses. The process is called clairvoyance and usually refers to visual impressions. People who see ghosts are clairvoyant whether the image is lifelike or merely a human-shaped fragment of a shadow. Visual information or impressions may include orbs, amorphous clouds, or objects. Since clairvoyance is limited to "real-time" events, any visual experience suggests that a ghost is present at the moment.

Retrocognition: Perception of visual impressions of events or places from the past is a form of clairvoyance called retrocognition. Psychic Derek Acora dramatically portrayed his retrocognition ability during ghost investigations in the popular TV show *Most Haunted*. If you watched my TV show *Ghosts of the Queen Mary*, you've seen me perform retrocognition. The most famous case of retrocognition was reported by two teachers, Charlotte Moberly and Eleanor Jourdain, after they visited the Petit Trianon at the Palace of Versailles in France in 1901. Known as the Moberly-Jourdain incident, the women reportedly witnessed people dressed in seventeenth-century clothing and structures that no longer existed. Their detailed descriptions of the experience, published in their 1911 book *An Adventure*, matched obscure historical records suggesting that the retrocognitive experience was genuine. Detailed accounts of the Moberly-Jourdain incident can be found online.

Psychometry: Information about an object or one of its users may be obtained by psychically gifted or skilled people through psychometry. First described in 1842 by Joseph R. Buchanan, the process has been used in séances, ghost hunts, and crime scene investigations. After a few minutes of handling an object, psychometry practitioners get visual impressions or become aware of information that cannot be the result of logical inference (piecing things together from clues you might have). Ghost hunters can use psychometry to gain information about a spirit's affinity for a chair or a book or why it moves a particular glass or key. Any object that has reportedly been moved by a ghost should be examined by psychometry. Investigators may get clues about the identity of the ghost or reasons for its haunting activity.

Retrieval of information by psychometry may be possible because of changes in an object's electromagnetic field (EMF) created by users. Repetitive handling of an object by its owner may alter its EMF and leave durable traces of the user's energy, much like a fingerprint, especially if intense emotions were associated with frequent use. A good example is my Civil War cavalry saber that was used in several battles. Psychometrists who handle the saber become aware of fear, rage, and remorse and perceive the image of a middle-aged Union army officer.

ORGANIZATION AND PREPARATION

It is not necessary to believe in spirits or paranormal phenomena in order to see a ghost or experience haunting activities. Indeed, most reports of ghost activities are made by unsuspecting people who never gave the matter much thought. But you should not include people in your group who openly express negative attitudes about these things. If you include skeptics, be sure that they agree to maintain an open mind and participate in a positive group attitude.

Keep your group small, limited to four members if possible. Ghosts have been seen by large groups of people, but small groups are more easily managed and likely to be of one mind in terms of objectives and methods.

Meet an hour or more prior to starting the ghost hunt at a location away from the site. Review the history of the ghost you seek and the previous reports of ghost activity at the site. Discuss the group's expectations based on known or suspected ghostly activity or specific research goals. Review any available reports of audio phenomena, still or video images, and visual apparitions and decide what methods would be optimal for recording these phenomena during your investigation.

Most importantly, agree to a plan of action if a sighting is made by any member of the group. The first priority for a ghost hunter is to maintain visual or auditory contact without a lot of activity such as making notes. Without breaking contact, do the following: activate recording devices; redirect audio, video, or photographic equipment to focus on the ghost; move yourself to the most advantageous position for listening or viewing the ghostly activity; and attract the attention of group members with a code word, hand signal (for example, touch the top of your head), or any action that signals other hunters so they can pick up your focus of attention.

Should you attempt to interact with the ghost? Do so only if the ghost invites you to speak or move. Often, a ghost hunter's movement or noise frightens the ghost or interferes with the perception of the apparition.

SEARCHING FOR GHOSTS

There are no strict rules or guidelines for successful ghost hunting except for one: be patient! Professional ghost hunters sometimes conduct investigations over a period of several days, weeks, or even months before achieving contact with a ghost. Others have observed full-body apparitions when they least expected it, while concentrating fully on some other activity. Regardless of the depth of your research or preparation, you need to be patient. The serious ghost hunter will anticipate that several trips to a haunted site may be required before some sign of ghostly activity is observed.

If you are ghost hunting with others, it may be advantageous to station members of your group at various places in the ghost's haunting grounds and use a reliable system to alert others to spirit activity. An audio signal can often reduce the need for monitoring other ghost hunters for hand signals. Equally important for a group is to establish a method for calling other hunters who may be some distance away, as when each member patrols a different portion of the site. Mechanical devices called "crickets" and flashes from a penlight may be effective. Hand-held radios or walkie-talkies and cellphones may also be used in some circumstances, but their electronic signals may trigger other ghost hunting devices.

Remaining stationary within a room, grave site, courtyard, or other confirmed location is often most productive. If a ghost is known to have a favorite chair, bed, or other place within a room, it will appear. Under these conditions, the patient ghost hunter will have a successful hunt. If your ghost is not known to appear at a specific place within a room or an outdoors area, position yourself to gain the broadest view of the site. A corner of a room is optimal because it allows the ghost unobstructed motion about the place while avoiding the impression of a trap set by uninvited people who occupy its favorite space. If you are outdoors at a grave site, for instance, position yourself at the base of a tree or in the shadows of a monument to conceal your presence while affording a view of your ghost's location. If your ghost is a mobile spirit, moving throughout a house, over a bridge, or about a courtyard or graveyard, you may have no choice but to move around the area. Search for a place where you feel a change in the thickness of the air or a cold spot or detect a peculiar odor.

Once you are on site, the aforementioned meditation methods may help you focus and maintain empathy for your ghost and enable you to effectively use psychic methods of investigation. Investigate sounds, even common sounds, as the ghost attempts to communicate with you. Make mental notes of the room temperature, air movement, and the sensations of abrupt change in atmosphere as you move about the site. Changes in these factors may indicate the presence of a ghost. Pay attention to your own sensations or perceptions, such as the odd feeling that someone is watching you, standing close by, or touching you. Your ghost may be hunting you!

WHAT TO DO WITH A GHOST

On occasion, professional ghost hunters make contact with a ghost by entering a trance and establishing two-way communications. The ghost hunter's companions hear him or her speak, but the ghost's voice can only be heard by the trance communicator. Sylvia Brown's book *Adventures of a Psychic* describes several of these trance communication sessions. Most ghost encounters are brief with little opportunity to engage the entity in conversation. But the ghost may make gestures or acknowledge your presence through eye contact, a touch on the shoulder, a sound, or a movement of an object. The ghost hunter must decide whether or not to follow the gestures or direction of a ghost.

Visitors to the Bay Area's historic haunted islands may feel the touch or tug of a ghost on their arm or shoulder. Spirits of deceased sailors, shipyard workers, sailors, marines, victims of disasters, or criminals may be trying to get living souls to notice them, move out of their way, or follow them to some important destination.

Phantom sailors aboard the World War II aircraft carrier USS *Hornet*, in Alameda, have been spotted in the chapel, sick bay, the hangar deck, the captain's bridge, forward anchor chain locker, and the engine room. Some of them beckon to visitors as if they expect startled ghost hunters to lend a hand in running the ship. At San Francisco's Maritime Park, a suicidal woman runs the length of the ferryboat *Eureka* before disappearing. Nearby, crew members of the 1880s square-rigged *Balclutha* generate intense cold spots where fatal accidents occurred.

On Alcatraz Island, the negative energy of former inmates is too much for some visitors. Many cannot enter some of the prison cells or the prison's hospital or tolerate even a short visit to the guard stations of cell block D. Disembodied screams, running footsteps, the crashing sound of heavy doors slamming shut, and intense sensations of rage have caused some anxious visitors to leave the tour and head for the dock.

The idea of a close experience with a ghost is frightening to most of us. More often, the ghost's activities are directed at getting the intruder to leave a room, house, or a ship. If you sense that your ghost wants you to leave, most hunters believe it is best not to push your luck. When you have established the nature of the ghost activity, ascertained that your companions have experienced the activity, taken a few digital images, and run your audio recorder for a few minutes, it may be time to leave. An experience with an unfriendly ghost can be disturbing.

Appendix

TV Shows, Videos, and Movies Featuring the Islands

TV SHOWS

Alcatraz. 1 season, 13 episodes. Aired in 2014. Fictional crime drama.
Dead Files. "Special Investigation: Alcatraz." Season 12, aired March 19, 2012.
Ghost Adventures. "Albion Castle." Season 1, episode 19, aired November 2, 2019.
———. "Alcatraz." Season 8, episode 9, aired October 11, 2013.
———. "Angel Island." Season 25, episode 1, aired October 4, 2023.
———. "Union Hotel (Benicia)." Season 18, episode 11, aired July 6, 2019.
———. "USS *Hornet*." Season 4, episode 7, aired November 5, 2010.
Ghost Hunters. "Alcatraz Live." Season 6, episode 1, aired March 3, 2010.
Ghost Lab. "Alcatraz." Season 1, episode 10, aired December 3, 2009.

YOUTUBE VIDEOS

"Alameda—The Island City." YouTube. https://youtu.be/jCMvOiupDLo?si=oKigt0_Y8BEn11ek.
"Angel Island State Park." YouTube. https://youtu.be/u90ikUDpgMM?si=L0a8YML4swJjGcFp.
"Good-Bye Treasure Island—San Francisco, 1940." YouTube. https://youtu.be/AfeZMRnRLYs?si=aq73J2oMvOm14vvJ.

"The Haunted Bay: Eagles Hall." YouTube. https://youtu.be/PSUYJ2BzuJE?si=W9jekjkeqcBGYwJp.
"Historic Alameda, 1920–1938." YouTube. https://youtu.be/Ssn_79ru9NQ?si=GUw2tC-lYb1sK1GP.
"History of Angel Island Immigration Station." YouTube. https://youtu.be/kvqtCo—Prs?si=rgm0OLTq0AOijzTY.
"History of Yerba Buena Island." YouTube. https://youtu.be/OZTbWeyWn8I?si=N8MG6oxamKLVr57f.
"The Immigrants of Angel Island." YouTube. https://youtu.be/wkKBZ8aEeLY?si=XVC46SxWMIAC9E2w.
"Mare Island Naval Shipyard V8." YouTube. https://youtu.be/Fx8OxY3XunM?si=7Hh6DS7hkpmrks8m.
"Mare Island Sky Tour, 1992." YouTube. https://youtu.be/XVjTFqZl_sk?si=p35J_8IJaJZMKEvh.
"Tour of the Nimitz House on Yerba Buena Island." YouTube. https://youtu.be/MxIAkV5N1PA?si=kthnzACkHLOSfZGW.
"Visit and Enjoy Treasure Island." YouTube. https://youtu.be/f0MyHSZrPxU?si=6UCQlu4wIZN1AMSs.
"What's It Like to Visit Mare Island?" YouTube. https://youtu.be/_t8XaY-eTwA?si=7Bp4FNQmlANNsidC.

The following movies are not about history or ghosts, but they are worth watching before visiting the Bay Area islands. They will give you a sneak preview of some of the scenery and a bit of local culture.

The Birdman of Alcatraz. Directed by John Frankenheimer. Starring Burt Lancaster. 1962.
Dirty Harry. Directed by Don Siegel. Starring Clint Eastwood. 1971.
Just Like Heaven. Directed by Mark Waters. Starring Reese Witherspoon and Mark Ruffalo. 2005.
The Pursuit of Happyness. Directed by Gabriele Muccino. Starring Will Smith and Jaden Smith. 2006.
The Rock. Directed by Michael Bay. Starring Nicolas Cage and Sean Connery. 1996.
Vertigo. Directed by Alfred Hitchcock. Starring James Stewart and Kim Novak. 1958.
Zodiac. Directed by David Fincher. Starring Jake Gyllenhaal and Mark Ruffalo. 2007.

Suggested Reading

Allison, Ross, and J. Temples. *Ghostology 101: Becoming a Ghost Hunter*. Author House, 2005.

Auerbach, Loyd. *ESP, Hauntings, and Poltergeists*. Warner Books, 1986.

———. *Ghost Hunting: How to Investigate the Paranormal*. Ronin Publishing, 2004.

———. *A Paranormal Casebook: Ghost Hunting in the New Millennium*. Atriad Press, 2005.

Auerbach, Patrick. *Alcatraz: The Surprising History of America's Most Notorious Prison*. CreateSpace Independent Publishing, 2016.

Bagans, Zak. *Ghost Hunting for Dummies*. For Dummies Publications, 2019.

Baldwin, Ronald. *The Ghosts of Alcatraz*. Independently published, 2024.

Bellanger, Michelle. *The Ghost Hunter's Survival Guide: Protection Techniques for Encounters with the Paranormal*. Llewellyn Publications, 2009.

Coustier, C., S. Marino, and K. Zimmerman. *True Ghost Stories of Alameda: The Hidden Side of the Island City*. InstantPublisher, 2005.

Davis, Bob. *Ghosts and Legends of Alcatraz*. The History Press, 2019.

Dutcher, Greta. *Alameda*. Arcadia Publishing, 2009.

Dwyer, Jeff. *America's Haunted Prisons and Jails: A Ghost Hunter's Guide*. CreateSpace Independent Publishing, 2019.

———. *The Art and Science of Paranormal Investigation*. Independently published, 2019.

———. *Ghost Hunter's Guide to the San Francisco Bay Area*. Rev. ed. Pelican Publishing, 2021.

———. *Psychic: Use Your Psychic Power to Experience Ghosts*. CreateSpace Independent Publishing, 2013.

Freeman, Haroldene. *Alcatraz, My Hometown: A Memoir of My Childhood Growing Up on the "Rock."* American Ghost Media, 2019.

Garbe, Suzanne. *Ghosts of Alcatraz and Other Hauntings of the West*. Capstone Press, 2021.

Hauck, Dennis William. *Haunted Places: The National Directory*. Penguin Group, 2002.

Hawes, Jason, Grant Wilson, and Michael Jan Friedman. *Ghost Hunting: True Stories of Unexplained Phenomenon from the Atlantic Paranormal Society*. Pocket Publishers, 2007.

Holzer, Hans. *Ghosts I've Met*. Barnes and Noble Books, 2005.

Larkins, William. *Alameda Naval Air Station*. Arcadia Publishing, 2010.

Morita, Drew. *Dead Men of Alcatraz: Profiles of the Prisoners and Guards Who Died at the Penitentiary*. CreateSpace Independent Publishing, 2019.

Newman, Richard. *Ghost Hunting for Beginners: Everything You Need to Know to Get Started*. Llewellyn Publications, 2011.

Richards, Rand. *Haunted San Francisco*. Heritage House Publishers, 2004.

Roddam, Brooks. *Mare Island*. IF SF Publishing, 2016.

Sweet, Charlotte. *How to Photograph the Paranormal*. Hampton Roads Publishing, 2004.

Van Praagh, James. *Ghosts Among Us: Uncovering the Truth About the Other Side*. HarperOne, 2009.

Veronico, Nicholas. *World War II Shipyards by the Bay*. Arcadia Publishing, 2007.

Wellman, Gregory. *History of Alcatraz Since 1853*. Arcadia Publishing, 2022.

Wlodarski, Robert, and Anne Wlodarski. *California Hauntspitality*. Whitechapel Productions, 2002.

INDEX

P

R

S

T

U

V

Y

Z